THE ESSENTIAL RUDHYAR

An outline and an evocation by

Leyla Rael Rudhyar

Raven Dreams Press

Boulder, CO

Published in 2024 by Raven Dreams Press
3980 Broadway Ste. 103 #186
Boulder, CO 80304
www.ravendreamspress.com

Copyright © 1983 by Leyla Rael Rudhyar

All rights reserved. No part of this publication may be reproduced or transmitted in any form or by any means, electronic or mechanical, including mimeographing, recording, taping, scanning, via Internet download, or by any information storage and retrieval systems, without permission in writing from Raven Dreams Press.

Reviewers may quote brief passages.
ISBN 979-8-9898397-2-8

Cover art by Tony Milner
Cover layout by Kam Bains
Printed in the United States of America

CONTENTS

I. FOUNDATIONS 1

   1. EXPERIENTIAL: The Cycle/The Seed 1
   2. PHILOSOPHICAL: Oriental Philosophies
      and Theosophy 3

II. CONCEPTUAL FORMULATIONS 5

   1. The Experience of Change 6
   2. Wholes in Time: Cycles 6
   3. Wholes in Space: Entities 8
   4. Wholeness 8
   5. Holarchy and Dharma 9
   6. Evolution and the Two-Way
      Cosmic Process 10
   7. The Challenge of "Transfinite" Wholeness
      to Finite Wholes 11
   8. Activity and Consciousness 12
   9. The Principles of Unity and Multiplicity 13
  10. The Movement of Wholeness 14
  11. The Cycle of Being 15
  12. Human Evolution and Reincarnation within
      the Cycle of Being 21

- 13. The Constitution and Entire Cycle of
     Human Being 28
- 14. The Nature and Function of Mind 32
- 15. The Planetary Whole and the Place and
     Function of Human Evolution Within It 35
- 16. Rhythms of Culture and Civilization 37
- 17. The Process of Transformation 39
- 18. Transpersonal Activity 40
- 19. The Process of Deconditioning and Renewal ... 41

III. RUDHYAR'S INTEGRATION OF EXPERIENCE AND CONCEPTS 43

- 1. The Arts 43
    - Poetry 45
    - Literature 48
    - Music 49
    - Painting 59
- 2. Astrology 64
- 3. Psychology 82

APPENDIX I:
Selected Poems 99

APPENDIX II:
Bibliography 107

I.

FOUNDATIONS

1. EXPERIENTIAL: THE CYCLE/THE SEED

Dane Rudhyar was born in Paris, France, on March 23, 1895, into a middle-class family of Norman and Celtic ancestry. His youth was marred only by ill health, which led in 1908 to a life-threatening operation that removed his left kidney and adrenal gland, and the sudden, untimely death of his father in 1911. The period of convalescence following surgery permitted his nascent mind and imagination to develop in peaceful solitude. At the age of sixteen, shortly after his father's death, he had an intuitive realization of the cyclic nature of all existence – of all natural organisms and especially cultures and their artistic manifestations. He felt that the European culture was passing through the "autumnal" phase of its cycle, and that the music of Debussy particularly represented the poignant but ephemeral and decadent beauty of such a phase. The outbreak of World War I was for him an "equinoctial storm" confirming his intuition.

From Rudhyar's point of view, then and now, any person living at such a time faces a basic choice. That is, symbolically speaking, he or she can identify himself or herself either with "the realm of the leaves" – with the glowing, but soon decaying, products of the ending cycle – or with the small, inconspicuous seeds that hold the promise of new life the following "spring." To identify oneself with the "realm of the seed" means to utterly dedicate oneself to the new life of one's species by condensing within oneself the "harvest" of one's natal, but dying, culture; to sever oneself from that culture and become self-sufficient, yet open to a basic "mutation," and to work to lay the symbolic and conceptual foundations for a new cycle of culture when conditions for it are right.

Rudhyar's choice was "seedhood." In 1916, as soon as he became twenty-one, he left Paris, severed himself as completely as possible from his natal French culture, language, family, mental conditioning, and name, and came to America. He identified himself as "a seed blown across the ocean... to sow itself in the fertile, virgin soil of a 'New World.'" In realizing the symbolic nature of his intuitions and acts, he also realized the significance of symbols: far from being "unreal" they constitute the root-reality affecting the mentality and behavior of human beings. In America in the 1920s and 30s, he tried to promote the idea of a "new American civilization" – to which no one responded. The "winds" of prevailing opinion held against the "seed": there was only Civilization (with a capital C – Western Civilization), and it was what came at the end of the long, linear march of "Progress" having started with "barbarism." The "New World" seemed to offer only rocky, unreceptive ground.

Yet the seed, too, was unready. It contained certain innate faculties which could be used constructively only when their function and field of operation became clear. Rudhyar had to pass through periods of inner development, severe testing, and maturation. Ambivalent experiences could be used constructively, but of course they need not. He also had to find some connection with the new ground, America – a way to make an impression, to become known.

The initial way was music. Rudhyar came to America as a composer of orchestral and piano music and as a writer of books and articles about music. He wrote about the music and musicians of the time he knew and also about Eastern music, which then was totally unknown and unappreciated in the West. Later on, when his musical endeavors were made futile by the Great Depression, the Neoclassical movement, and World War II, the field of astrology opened as an unsought avenue of contact with the American consciousness. Yet whether the means be music or astrology, what Rudhyar had to bring could be explained and understood only on the basis of a new philosophical outlook which took many years to mature fully. It started in 1917 with a daily study of books at the New York Public Library.

2. PHILOSOPHICAL: EASTERN PHILOSOPHIES AND THEOSOPHY

Between 1917 and 1928, Rudhyar made an in-depth study of occult and various Eastern philosophies (he always stresses that Hindu philosophy in particular is not monolithic, the Indian subcontinent having produced many types of philosophy, some almost entirely materialistic, others focusing almost entirely on transcendent realities). His studies confirmed his early intuition about the importance and universality of cycles. The *Secret Doctrine* of H. P. Blavatsky especially laid the foundations for much of his later philosophical development.

But Rudhyar did not study theosophy and Eastern philosophies to accumulate a mass of scholarly data or interesting "information." Through his studies he consciously tried to develop a new type of mind able to deal with universal, spiritual, and metaphysical principles and cyclic processes. He came to definitely feel that his dharma (destiny or truth-of-being) would be to reformulate ancient and traditional metaphysical and occult concepts in terms that would both nourish the development of, and be understandable by, this kind of mind, which he calls "the mind of wholeness," through a process which he calls "clairthinking" – the direct experience of ideas.

While he studied a vast number of books and met an impressive list of notable personalities, Rudhyar has (to date) remained isolated from the mainstream of official and academic thought. Between 1933 and 1968, his work in reformulating astrology along humanistic and transpersonal lines has been his main contact, not so much with his own generation as with succeeding ones. Yet his astrological work cannot be understood fully unless it is seen within the context of the basic philosophy and metaphysics he formulated in his books *The Planetarization of Consciousness* (1970) and *Rhythm of Wholeness* (1982), and more partially, yet specifically, in other works starting with *Art as Release of Power* (1929), and ending with *Occult Preparations for a New Age* (1974), *Culture, Crisis and Creativity* (1976), and *Beyond Individualism* (1977), none of which refer to astrology.

II.

CONCEPTUAL FORMULATIONS

As a philosopher, Rudhyar's intent has been to formulate, as inclusively as he could, a "new" frame of reference for understanding what it means to be human – especially in a time of crisis and potential transformation such as we are passing through today – not to establish a dogma or "school" of philosophy, per se. He has tried to formulate a set of evocative and consistent images enabling individuals, who are ready, to take the next step in their evolution, as individuals, as members of the Euro-American culture, and as participants in the actualization of the human potential on the planet earth. In relation to the way human consciousness has developed during the two millennia of Western civilization, his work follows the precedent set by the founders of the six great Schools (*darshanas*) of Indian philosophies, and of other Asian systems having behavioral, psychological, and mental implications and applications: each system addressed the level of consciousness and the biopsychic needs of a particular type or class of human beings and represented a practical, realistic way for them to reach the next possible evolutionary condition. Each system (and its practical application) was offered to persons ready and eager to transcend the limitations of the culture which had formed their minds and patterns of behavior.

1. THE EXPERIENCE OF CHANGE

For Rudhyar, the experience of change is the most fundamental of all human experiences. His philosophy and approach to psychology studies the way the experience of change gives rise to the awareness of repetitive changes, to the sense of time, and to the entitizing of repeated changes into persons and objects.

The experience of repetitive changes leads to the awareness that time is cyclic – that is, that it operates in units integrating a multiplicity of activities and events. The experience of repeated relations with the sources of changes gives rise to the realization of wholes in space – both to the awareness of objective wholes to which the experiencer is related, and to the experiencer's subjective realization of being a whole himself or herself. Space is the generalization and abstraction of this experience of relationship.

2. WHOLES IN TIME: CYCLES

Existence implies activity and change; cycles are series of ordered changes. A cycle is a whole in time having a defined beginning, middle (culmination), and end. It begins in a "seed condition," with a release of potentialities which will be actualized (at least to some extent) during the "spring" and "summer" quarters of the cycle. The culmination of the cycle, its symbolic "flowering," reveals its harvest of positive accomplishment, its failure to actualize some potentialities, and the byproducts and waste of its course of development. During its "autumnal" and "winter" phases, new "seeds" are formed, out of which a new cycle will proceed the following "spring," while "leaves" (inevitable byproducts) decay to provide raw materials for the new cycle. The next cycle (be it cosmic or personal) proceeds in answer to the need of these raw materials to be given a "second chance" for harmonious embodiment.

While succeeding cycles proceed according to the same pattern, which is characteristic of all cycles, whatever their scope or level of operation, the contents of two cycles are never the same. This is because the relatedness of the multiplicity of factors operating within a cycle introduces an element of unpredictability or indeterminacy. Hence, for Rudhyar, there can be no Nietzschean eternal return; cycles follow and build upon one another in a spirallic way. Moreover, for him:

> The concept of the cycle is at least potentially the most inclusive of all symbols, because it constitutes a frame of reference for all symbols [and experiences]; it enables us to situate, and to give a structural meaning, to any and all symbols [and experiences]. It answers, perhaps, to the most profound need of the human mind, the need to harmonize, within an intelligible pattern of order and significance, ideas and beliefs, modes of feeling and behaving, which, though radically different, must be granted an objective and historical-geographical value. (*Planetarization of Consciousness*, p. 238)

3. WHOLES IN SPACE: ENTITIES

While cycles structure the processes of existence in time, existence manifests spatially in wholes – limited fields of interrelated functional activities. Wholes are "cyclocosms"; they have boundaries in time (a life cycle or span of existence) and in space (cosmos = a life-field).

Integrating the multiplicity of elements and functions of all existential wholes is a principle of unity, ONE or SELF (Rudhyar normally uses these words with all letters capitalized). In *The Planetarization of Consciousness*, he calls it the Principle of Wholeness and likens it to the Hindu principle *atman*: in itself ONE is nothing (no thing) and does nothing, yet without it nothing (no whole) could exist.

4. WHOLENESS

For Rudhyar, "Wholeness is the ultimate idea we can have of the meaning of being...Wholeness is the beingness of all wholes."

To be is to be a whole, unfolding its inherent potentialities through cycles of changes (time) and in a state of unceasing relatedness to other wholes (space). All **wholes** are, and must be, by definition, finite. But **Wholeness** is not finite, because it applies to all wholes and is not limited to any particular whole or condition of being. Yet neither is Wholeness infinite, because the concept of infinity (to which human beings usually attach a powerful emotional charge) is only one pole of an intellectual dualism whose other pole is finitude. All wholes are finite, but Wholeness is undefinable. The most that can be said of it is that it is "transfinite" in the sense that it can only "be" through wholes – any and all kinds of wholes operating at any and all levels of wholeness. The universe is a hierarchy of wholes, a hierarchy of levels of wholeness.

5. HOLARCHY AND DHARMA

Rudhyar has coined the term **holarchy** to refer to this hierarchy of wholes within wholes within wholes…cycles within cycles within cycles. It is a hierarchy of containment, not (as in governmental, corporate, and military hierarchies) of command.

Lesser (less inclusive) wholes [or cycles] operate within greater (more inclusive) wholes [cycles], and greater wholes [cycles] regulate the activities and rhythms of lesser wholes [cycles], each of which, by performing a function within the greater whole [cycle] of which it is a differentiated part (but also a whole), actualizes an aspect of the greater whole [cycle]. This actualization constitutes the **dharma** (destiny or truth-of-being) of the lesser whole.

Two types of relationship thus operate within the holarchic universe:

1) **vertical relationships** between lesser wholes and greater wholes of which they are a part, the wholeness of the greater whole (its activity and consciousness) including the wholeness (activity and consciousness) of the lesser whole; and
2) **horizontal relationships** between wholes operating at the same level.

6. EVOLUTION AND THE TWO-WAY COSMIC PROCESS

While other thinkers (for example, Smuts, Whyte, Koestler, von Bertalanffy, Laszlo) have recognized that the universe is a hierarchy of wholes evolving to form increasingly complex and refined systems of organization and states of being – atoms, molecules, cells, organs, organisms – Rudhyar differs from such thinkers in three ways:

1) While Smuts and Jung considered the present day human condition (which they called "Personality") to be the apex or ultimate product of evolution – the "highest" or most complex, most refined, and most sensitive whole – Rudhyar believes that mankind is still "in the making," still responding to a process of evolution which, in time, will transfigure humanity and lead it to realize a transhuman stage.

2) Rudhyar sees no logical reason not to extend the evolutionary sequence to include species, human cultures, planets, solar systems, galaxies, and so on. For Rudhyar, a society and its culture form an integrated whole (a culture-whole) operating primarily at a psychic level (as a psychic organism) through religious and secular symbols, images, assumptions, and paradigms. Most importantly, he considers the earth as the physical body of a planetary whole, Terra (or Gaia), also operating and evolving at psychic, mental, and spiritual levels.

3) In contrast to the one-directional picture of evolution presented not only by Darwin and his West-

ern predecessors and successors, but also in ancient India ("I was a stone, I became a plant," and so on), Rudhyar stresses the reality of a "two-way" process integrating the "descent" or **involution** of spiritual archetypes (principles, forms, and formulas of organization) and a synchronous "ascent" or **evolution** (a progressive complexification and refinement) of material substances and systems coming to embody these archetypes.

If Rudhyar has called this twofold process of involution evolution a "two-way evolution," it is because both movements – the involutionary "descent" of unitarian spirit and integrative forms of organization, and the evolutionary "ascent" or progressive refinement of material systems – imply a process of differentiation. It can be considered only one process according to which a principle of Unity gradually yields to a principle of Multiplicity (see sections 9, 10, and 11 below).

7. THE CHALLENGE OF "TRANSFINITE" WHOLENESS TO FINITE WHOLES

The question raised by the concept of a hierarchical series of wholes is, can one conceive of an end to the series? Is there a greatest whole of which there would be no greater? Similarly, is there an ultimately "smallest" whole? For Rudhyar, this is only an intellectual and abstract problem, because living experience presents to human beings only **levels of wholeness** – spheres and conditions of being which are, to some degree, higher (more inclusive) or lower (less inclusive) than the ones in which human beings function. Only the intellectual mind ever deals with the abstract possibility of "greatest" or "smallest," neither of which has realistic meaning. For Rudhyar, reality is where one stands, and it is inevitably conditioned and limited by the level at which one operates. Nevertheless, the wholeness in any whole can "resonate" to the wholeness in any other whole (although the resonating whole's experience of the wholeness of the greater whole is still conditioned by its own level of wholeness).

Thus, for Rudhyar, the challenge facing human beings is to experience the plenitude or fullness of wholeness of being at the human level; to try to understand the meaning of the human condition in relation to the greater wholes human beings can experience, and to take the next step in human evolution that is possible at the time one lives – not to chase after intellectual phantoms seeming to promise escape from the fact of being a finite whole operating at the human level.

8. ACTIVITY AND CONSCIOUSNESS

While recent and contemporary psychologies and philosophies often stress consciousness as the primary ground of being, Rudhyar's approach differs from them in that he considers consciousness indissolubly associated with, and the concomitant of, **activity**.

For him, a living being is a whole – an organized system of activity within definite limits – and activity within such an organized system generates consciousness. Each level of organization – thus of wholeness – implies a particular type of consciousness as well as activity: there is consciousness in an atom, a planet, and a galaxy, as well as in a human being, because each is an organized system of activity, a consistent and evolving whole.

In other words, consciousness is the subjective side of activity, and activity is the objective side of consciousness. Thus, all wholes are both active and conscious. The activity and consciousness of a greater whole encompasses and includes the activity and consciousness of the lesser wholes it contains. Every whole is simultaneously an experiencing subject and an object to other subjects; every "one" is part of the category of "many" for other "ones."

9. THE PRINCIPLES OF UNITY AND MULTIPLICITY

From the interplay of involution and evolution, consciousness and activity, subjectivity and objectivity, oneness and manyness, Rudhyar derives two principles inherent and co-active in Wholeness: the **principle of Unity** and the **principle of Multiplicity**. In Chinese philosophy they are called Yin and Yang (and Rudhyar's philosophical approach is perhaps closer in spirit to Chinese than to Hindu Metaphysics, although it includes elements from both).

Because of the principle of Unity, motion (activity) is rhythmic and cyclic (occurring in units), and existence manifests in wholes. Because of the principle of Multiplicity, existence manifests as a multitude of whole in which ever more expansion and differentiation occurs. Because of the principle of Unity, the process of differentiation (evolution) is self-actualizing – that is, it is guided from within by and toward the actualization of a set of inherent (involutionary) archetypal principles.

10. THE MOVEMENT OF WHOLENESS

As the primary fact of human experience is change, the relationship between the principles of Unity and Multiplicity is dynamic and ceaselessly changing. Rudhyar calls it the **Movement of Wholeness**. Like Yin and Yang within the symbol Tai Chi, the principle of Unity waxes as the principle of Multiplicity wanes and vice versa. Neither can ever totally overpower the other and absolutely control the Movement. Each principle can only attain a maximum of relative predominance; as soon as either principle achieves this maximum strength, the trend of the Movement reverses itself and the other principle surges back and begins to rise.

Hence, for Rudhyar, there can be no absolute subjectivity, no absolute Subject, "the One." Neither can there be absolute multiplicity: if no principle of Unity were in operation, there could be no unity of being, only an undifferentiated, infinite extension of nameless substance; no experiencing subjects because no wholes with defining boundaries, no experiences because no experiencers.

When the principle of Multiplicity is stronger than the principle of Unity, being (that is, activity and consciousness) is more objective than subjective; when the principle of unity predominates, being is predominantly subjective.

CONCEPTUAL FORMULATIONS 15

11. THE CYCLE OF BEING

The most fundamental metaphysical question is, why is there a universe? In other words, why is there anything (being) instead of nothing (nonbeing)? The religious mind asks, why did God (or spirit in a nonpersonal sense) create the universe? The typical Hindu answer is that creation is the Play (*lila*) of Brahman. Christian theology speaks instead of a divine Plan whereby God creates the universe out of nothing and reveals the fullness of his divinity to his creatures; within this Plan, original sin causes God to reveal his immense compassion by sacrificing his one and only Son to redeem sinful humanity. Modern science offers the scenario of an originating Big Bang, and a subsequent process of evolution proceeding according to random motion and "natural law."

Rudhyar could never accept either the Plan of redemption or the divine Play idea, or the purposeless interplay of randomness and "law" (sans lawgiver). For him, as for the Hindu philosopher, existence is cyclic, whether one thinks of it in cosmic or in human terms. A cosmos (or a human being) is born in answer to a need, because the next step or phase of the Movement of Wholeness calls for it.

The dynamic interplay between the principles of Unity and Multiplicity within the Movement of Wholeness describes what Rudhyar calls the **cycle of being**. Realizing well the limitations of a graphic illustration, Rudhyar nevertheless presents the cycle of being as follows (see figure opposite).

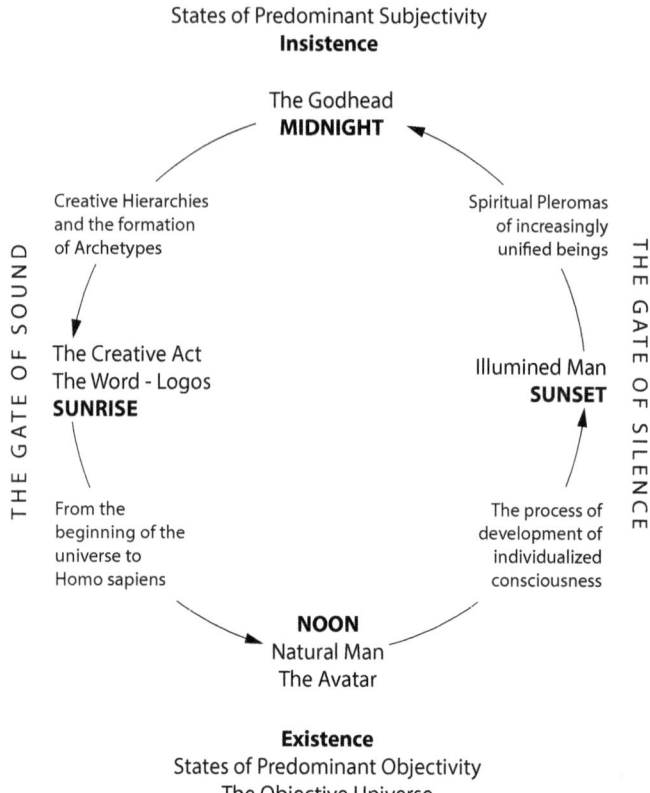

Four significant turning points and quadrants result from the cyclic and symmetrical motion of two opposite forces within a finite field of activity, one waxing as the other wanes. At two points in the cycle, the forces are of equal strength, with one definitely waxing and the other on the wane. At two others, one force reaches the maximum of its power while the other is as weak as it can be. The symbolism attached to the resulting turning points, hemicycles, and quadrants is based on the diurnal cycle, but one must keep in mind that in this application of it the "light" of day is never totally absent from the "darkness" of night and vice versa.

The cycle of being never begins or ends, but to talk about it, one has to choose a point at which to start. At the symbolic Sunrise, the principles of Unity and Multiplicity are in equilibrium, with the principle of Multiplicity waxing and beginning to surpass the strength of the principle of Unity. Cosmologically, this is Creation, the "birth" of a universe. Between the symbolic Sunrise and Sunset, the principle of Multiplicity is stronger than the principle of Unity. Hence, this Day hemicycle represents what we experience as the world of existence, which is dominated by objectivity, but which includes internalized subjective activities represented by the less powerful, but ever present, principle of Unity. (For a human being, Sunrise represents the moment of birth; Sunset, the death of the physical body.)

At the symbolic Sunset, the principles of Unity and Multiplicity are again of equal strength, but the principle of Unity, which has been waxing since the symbolic Noon, soon surpasses the strength of the principle of Multiplicity. The Night hemicycle from Sunset to Sunrise, during which the principle of Unity is stronger than the principle of Multiplicity, represents a condition of being which usually is spoken of in negative terms – nonbeing, nonexistence, nonmanifestation, changeless, timeless. For Rudhyar, however, these terms are unfortunate: the Movement of Wholeness is an all-inclusive and total affirmation of being; there can be no "nonbeing" in the "cycle of being." Hence, this half of the cycle represents a condition of predominantly subjective being dominated by subjective activity (which is not, however, "nonactivity"). As the principle of Multiplicity is never absolutely inoperative, this Night hemicycle implies a transphysical substance, less objective than physical matter – an increasingly subtle and homogenous (nondifferentiated) kind of matter. In contrast to the word **existence**, which applies to the Day hemicycle, Rudhyar has coined the term "**insistence**" to refer to the Night portion of the cycle.[1]

Sunrise symbolizes the state of potentiality in which a cycle of existence (which is one half of the total cycle of being) begins. It represents a "seed condition" (the "cosmic Egg"). This alpha condition is "form endowed with power." This power is the energy of the Movement of Wholeness itself. Religions refer to this power and condition as God, the Creator. For Rudhyar, however, God is not "outside" the Movement of Wholeness, which is truly all-inclusive (what could be "outside" of Wholeness?), but a phase of, and an action in, it (as is Man). This idea – seeing God and divine activity as a series of phases and states within the cycle of being – is indeed revolutionary. It may be the most striking idea Rudhyar has presented. He symbolizes this phase as unpersonifiably as possible by using the term **creative Word** or **Logos**.

The creative Word is formulated between Midnight and Sunrise by what Rudhyar calls the **divine Mind** – the predominantly subjective activity occurring when the principle

---

1 In relation to this Night period, the terms "hemicycle" and "half cycle" should not be interpreted quantitatively; they do not refer to a definite period of measurable time such as human beings experience in a physical, existential universe of moving celestial bodies. Objective, measurable time depends on the rhythm and apparent speed of objective activity to an experimenter differentiated from it. But time can be predominantly objective and measurable or predominantly subjective. In either case, it is the abstraction of the consciousness of motion – which is the "substance" of change – and motion is "eternal," that is, cyclic.

of Unity is stronger than the principle of Multiplicity, which is nevertheless waxing. This process refers to the activity of what religious and esoteric cosmogonies call creative Hierarchies of beings which build the archetypal foundations for the material universe.

From Sunrise to Noon, when the strength of the principle of Multiplicity is greater than that of the principle of Unity, the creative Word cyclically "descends" and differentiates (involution) into specific "Letters" which acquire an increasingly limited focus as **archetypes**. These principles, forms, and formulas of organization progressively relate to and structure synchronously evolving (responding, also differentiating) material substances and systems. This matter is the nearly (but not quite) absolute chaos of decayed waste products from the previous cycle. At first it is almost totally indifferent to principles of organization. As archetypes "descend" and differentiate, they organize and find material embodiment in gradually responding matter and material systems (atoms, galaxies, solar systems, planets), then in material organizations sufficiently complex, refined, and sensitive to respond at the level of organization we call **life**.

At the symbolic Noon, the principle of Multiplicity reaches its maximum strength. Differentiation "triumphs" when life produces the extremely complex, refined, and sensitive biological species Homo sapiens, which Rudhyar calls **Natural Man**. When protohuman beings begin to respond to the "descent" of truly human (that is, mental) archetypes, the process of human evolution begins.

It ends, and the entire cycle of being culminates, at the symbolic Sunset, in an omega condition fully actualizing the alpha condition symbolized by Sunrise. Rudhyar calls the state of perfection symbolized by Sunset **Illumined Man**. In relation to the human condition today, it is a state of superhuman or transhuman activity; in terms of the whole process of human evolution, it is the full actualization of the human potential – that is, of the archetype Man (Anthropos). Illumined Man is the planetary collectivity of beings who reach this state. Because the principles of Unity and Multiplicity are in equilibrium at the symbolic Sunset, differentiation of purpose, activity, and will balance oneness of consciousness in this collectivity.

After the symbolic Sunset, as the principle of Unity surpasses the strength of the principle of Multiplicity, this collectivity becomes increasingly unified and unanimous (literally, "of one soul"). Rudhyar refers to this state as the **Pleroma** – an old Gnostic term meaning fulfillment or plenitude of being. The Pleroma state evolves in a mostly subjective way, balancing, as it were, the period of material evolution of the cosmos (from Sunrise to Noon). There are Pleromas after Pleromas, each cosmically more inclusive than the other.

At the symbolic Midnight, this evolution reaches an almost (but not quite) static degree of subjectivity and oneness which Rudhyar calls the **Godhead** state. He does not speak of the Godhead as "the Absolute" as many mystics, philosophers, and theologians do; for him, if one can speak of "the Absolute" at all, the term would refer to Wholeness. Neither does he refer to this state of maximum unity and subjectivity as "Reality" in contrast to the "unreality" or "illusion" of the existential world: for Rudhyar, unity is no more "real" than multiplicity; reality is the cyclic interplay between them. Neither is the Godhead a supreme Being utterly transcendent and "external" to the cycle of being; like God, the Creator, it is a phase and an action in, and of, it.

Inherent in the nearly absolute oneness of the Godhead state is the all-inclusive compassion of Wholeness that compels a new universe to be, first, conceived, then (at the symbolic Sunrise) born (although time does not exist during the hemicycle of "*inistence*" – one can only say that it "*inists*" or that processes of change "endure"). For while the cycle of being culminates in the state of Illumined Man, all human beings do not reach this state; many partially or totally fail to actualize the potential inherent in the archetype Man. (Failure in most cases is only partial when seen in relation to perfection; it encompasses a continuum from total failure to almost perfection.) These failures are, as it were, built into the system. Those who reach perfection need them and are responsible for them: seeds awaiting germination during winter needed green leaves and flowers to be produced. Yet, inevitably, flowers and leaves wither and die and break down into humus from which they differentiate and from which future generations of plants will draw nourishment. The nearly (but not quite) absolute oneness of the Godhead state encompasses the responsibility for, and the need of, these by-products; their very presence ("inistence") calls forth the compassion of the Godhead to conceive of a new universe in which they will have a "second chance" to reach Illumination.

12. HUMAN EVOLUTION & REINCARNATION WITHIN THE CYCLE OF BEING

At the symbolic Noon of the cycle of being, life produces the biological species Homo sapiens – natural Man, the result of the "triumph" of the principle of Multiplicity over the principle of Unity, which is then at its lowest ebb. The resurgence of the principle of Unity represents a radical reversal of the Movement of Wholeness and refers to the beginning of the "descent" and focusing (involution) of a set of truly human (that is, mental) potentialities which Rudhyar calls Anthropos, the **archetype Man**. On the one hand, this archetype is inherent in the creative Word (Logos) beginning the existential process at Sunrise. On the other, beginning at the symbolic Noon, it is "fixed" into the "soil" of evolving earth-materials by a series of **avatars** acting as agents for the Movement of Wholeness and the "descending" archetype Man. These avatars also can be considered "projections" into the world of existence of the compassion of the Godhead state. They "graft" the potentiality for truly human development – mind and the potentiality of individual selfhood – onto the "stock" of Natural Man.

The beginning of this process is symbolized in the Greek myth of Prometheus, who bestowed the gift of divine fire (mind and the capacity for self-consciousness) on nascent mankind. Similarly, the traditions of India speak of the coming to earth of the *Kumaras* (also called *Agnishvattas*, vehicles of fire, and *Manasaputras*, progenitors of mind). Such an event is said to have occurred in the remotest past, presumably millions of years ago. Also mentioned are lesser avatars appearing throughout the ages. In successive epochs and periods (cycles within cycles within cycles, each of which, while a phase of the cycle of being, also passes through a complete cyclic pattern itself), successive avataric personages restate and reveal successive aspects of this mental potential. Rudhyar relates this process of mental fecundation to what he calls the **process of civilization** (see section 16 to follow).

While the beginning of this involutionary process is an "event" of planetary scope, the evolutionary aspect of it proceeds at different paces and places in different epochs. At first human evolution proceeds primarily collectively, through the development of a series of successive and simultaneous cultures which Rudhyar, in order to stress their objective and organic character, calls **culture-wholes**. Culture-wholes are born, mature, and disintegrate, much as biological organisms do; in the process, they leave a "seed harvest" and waste products (karma) to their successors.

On the one hand, culture-wholes are rooted in the particular climatic, geographic, and racial "soil" of a group of biologically related human beings, whose consciousness translates these environmental and biological characteristics into symbols. These symbols feed the development of what Rudhyar calls **collective psychism**. Collective psychism is to the integration of a culture what the life-force (*prana* or *chi*) is to a biological organism: a culture-whole is a psychic organism integrating and molding the activities and consciousness of its human members. At first, collective psychism is an "overtone" of the biological relatedness of the people; the members of the culture-whole develop a strongly exclusivistic attitude and consider anything that was not born within their life-space and of their bloodline, anything that does not act, feel, and think as they do, foreign and a potential enemy. Taboos and myths arise on the basis of collective experience and deeply felt needs; collective wholeness is projected and deified as the tribal ancestor or god.

On the other hand, such a unifying image embodies a spiritual impulse or archetype emanated through an agent for the archetype Man, an avatar. Such a figure or personage may be an aspect of the harvest of a previous cycle of culture, a "seed" in which a basic "mutation" (a "grafting" of a new aspect of the creative mental potential inherent in the archetype Man) has taken place. (Rudhyar refuses to discount the nearly universal traditions according to which divine kings or instructors brought language, agriculture, and the arts to nascent mankind; "seed being" summing up the harvest of a previously "flowering" cycle of culture would indeed seem "divine" to the relatively crude "raw materials" of a nascent culture-whole.) The avataric personage's deeds and teachings ("divine revelation") become the foundation for the developing culture's religion – its "collective soul" – which becomes a most powerful factor in the lives and psychomental development of its members.

Functioning within culture-wholes, human beings become what Rudhyar calls **persons**, "specimen" of a culture – that is, human beings whose minds, psyches, and behavior are molded by, and function almost totally within, the culture's collective psychism, within the taken-for-granted frame of reference of the culture's language, myths, symbols, images, religion, and way of life. For Rudhyar, without participation in a society and its culture, there can be no personhood; without active or passive participation in a culture-whole, a human being is merely a biological organism, a member of the species Homo sapiens with the potentiality for becoming a person – but potentiality is not actuality.

The behavior and consciousness of a person are structured and "managed" by an **ego** – which, for Rudhyar, is not an entity, but a set of functional activities. For him, the ego constitutes an interface and mechanism of adjustment between the human biological organism's instinct for survival and the psychosocial pressures of its cultural and family environment. The development of an ego presupposes the existence of both a powerful environment and a subjective principle seeking to manifest as personhood.

This principle, ONE or SELF, is the "presence" of the principle of Unity in the multiplicity-dominated existential organism. It is what is at the root of the "feeling-of-being-I" distinct from other "I"s. At the strictly biological level of human organization, it has an instinctual, generic character experienced as a sense of organic wholeness (the "wisdom of the body"); it manifests as a particular temperament (that is, as a quality of vitality associated with such biological factors as body type). At the psychosocial level, the ego develops a particular form according to the way the particular temperament interacts with prevailing psychosocial pressures, presumably also reflecting the individual subjective principle.

Eventually, as a culture-whole complexifies, and especially when it interacts with other culture-wholes structured by a different type of collective psychism and way of life, it begins to be affected by the process of **individualization**. Through the introduction of alien beliefs, concepts, and practices (via travel, commerce, conquest, or invasion) the integrity of the culture's collective psychism begins to break down and to lose its capacity to mold, hold together, and dominate the consciousness of its members. Persons of a rebellious or critical temperament, or whose egos have developed cynically or insecurely in reaction to the breakdown of cultural paradigms, mores, and norms, are the first to respond to this process – which is polarized and dynamized by an increasing "descent" and focusing of **spiritual Qualities**, which may be considered the many "Letters" of the original creative Word. These Qualities seek a one-to-one relationship with – and eventually total embodiment in – a sufficiently responsive human organism and individualized mind. As the process (involution-evolution) accelerates, individuals emerge from the cultural matrix. Their minds and wills become at least relatively autonomous and independent from both biological compulsion and collective cultural imperatives; they become increasingly able (potentially, that is) to respond to the spiritual Quality seeking eventually to manifest concretely through them.

The process of individualization, however, involves many dangers and pitfalls. It is inherently tragic and inevitably generates tension, conflict, strife, and a sense of isolation and alienation (*dukka* in Buddhist terminology, *angst* in German). As collective controls break down, and would-be individuals break free of them, the "individuals" clamor to "do their own thing." But more often than not, their "own" thing is merely a diametrical opposition to what they feel as binding collective forces. Their striving for "liberation" is usually an emotional, more or less blind, reaction of the ego seeking to emerge from the cultural womb – or, more ambiguously, to legitimize or even aggrandize itself in the eyes of a collective system it purportedly wants to repudiate.

Eventually, the process of individualization must lead to the **Path of transformation**. Sooner or later, individuals tire of conflict or realize its inherently self-defeating nature and results. Individuality must be seen as valuable only within a greater whole to which it contributes constructively. The individual may envision this greater whole as humanity or the planet earth, or he or she may relate it to the spiritual Quality (often called the "higher Self" in contrast to the personality or body/mind complex or "lower self") attempting to establish contact with him or her. For while the spiritual Quality represents the highest quality of individuality potential within a human being, because it is a highly differentiated "Letter" of the original creative Word it is an aspect of the greater whole Anthropos, the archetype Man.[2]

---

2 Archetypal Man, in turn, is a reflection of the Logos – according to some ancient philosophies, the "image and likeness of God." Yet this "image and likeness" is potential in mankind as a whole; it may not be actualizable in all newborn babies.

A spiritual Quality's attempt to establish a one-to-one relationship with an individualized person operates cyclically and constitutes, for Rudhyar, the true meaning of **"reincarnation."** In its process of differentiation, a spiritual Quality seeks and establishes various degrees of relationship with a series of human personalities, whose lives are linked in that they are all related to the same spiritual Quality. The process has as its goal, as its fully actualized symbolic Sunset, the total union or **"divine marriage"** of a spiritual Quality and a fully adequate individualized person totally embodying its meaning and function. Thus, from Rudhyar's point of view, reincarnation is not the periodic reappearance of the same person, nor is it actually reincarnation. Strictly speaking, from his point of view, there is only one full incarnation – the one that culminates in complete union, the "divine marriage."

Rudhyar believes that, collectively speaking, mankind today has reached a point about halfway between the symbolic Noon and Sunset of the present cycle of human development. Thus, the most significant factor operating in human evolution today is the gradual rise of the principle of Unity. It manifests, on the one hand, in an increasing individualization of human consciousness and activity in response to the increasing "descent" and focusing of spiritual Qualities; and on the other, as an increasing "planetarization" of it – that is an increasing capacity for human beings to be detached from a particular local space and cultural temperament and to operate (at least potentially and in consciousness) in terms of the whole planet earth.

Particular individuals (and cultures) may be "ahead of" or "behind" the "norm" defined by their position within a particular subcycle and sub-subcycle. Individuals significantly ahead of the collective pace already have reached the condition of Illumined Man. In their togetherness, they constitute what esoteric traditions call the White Lodge, which Rudhyar refers to as the **Pleroma** – the collectivity of illumined, formerly human beings whose centers of consciousness interpenetrate and resonate in unanimity of purpose but retain the individuality and functional nature of the particular spiritual Quality each represents. These illumined beings (Masters, Mahatmas, Elder Brothers of humanity) are always ready to guide, assist, and test those who seek to tread the Path of transformation leading to the state of Illumined Man and to the transindividual level of the Pleroma. Thus, for Rudhyar, while the Pleroma is a phase of the universal cycle of being, it is also now, and it is also in the making now. The dharma of all human beings is to aspire to participate in that making by becoming attuned to what is represented by the now definitely waxing principle of Unity.

13. THE CONSTITUTION AND ENTIRE CYCLE OF HUMAN BEING

The broadly cosmic and evolutionary interpretation of the cycle of being (the Movement of Wholeness) presented in sections 11 and 12 above does not preclude the pattern's application to the cycle of being of a particular human being during and after his or her bodily existence. It also has definite relevance to the 24-hour cycle of personal existence during waking and sleep. Each night in deep, dreamless sleep, the sleeper reaches a condition of relative Godhead; but in the daily personal existential cycle, the principle of Multiplicity and the power of objective existence as a biological organism is so strong that on awakening the sleeper has no remembrance of the moment of maximum subjectivity he or she reached in **consciousness** while his or her body was rebuilding its potential of organic **activity**. Neither does a human being "remember" the relative Godhead state of the slightly larger sub-subcycle of the cycle of being that resulted in the birth of a physical body he or she has come to identify as "mine."

Before the completion of the "divine marriage" between a fully differentiated and focused spiritual Quality and a fully adequate individualized human being, the spiritual Quality seeks to establish a one-to-one relationship with a series of human personalities, each of which is born, matures, and dies without having achieved total union with the spiritual Quality. The birth of a particular person represents that cyclic attempt's symbolic Sunrise; the death of his or her physical body refers to its symbolic Sunset. What occurs during the following Night hemicycle depends on the degree of differentiation of the spiritual Quality, on the degree or "closeness" of one-to-one relationship with it the personality could accept during life, and on the development of the different levels of activity and consciousness constituting the total human being.

For Rudhyar, the human being, archetypally considered, is threefold and is constituted by (a) an **objective physical** and superphysical (subtle or "etheric") body; (b) a **subjective spiritual** entity (the immanent or latent potentialities defined by the spiritual Quality) and (c) a highly complex **psychomental network** of functions providing the link and "vessel" necessary for the eventual (potential) integration of the spiritual and the material. Each of these three components can be considered threefold, as the other two levels are "reflected" in it.

Death means the (at least relative) disassociation and separation of these three basic principles, each of which follows its own course after death. The elements of the physical body return to the planetary field of matter and life-energy from which they differentiated. The elements of the psycho-mental network that had been dominated by collective psychism also "return" (an inadequate term not to be taken literally) to the collective psychic field from which they had been drawn. They are what "psychics" and "mediums" usually contact of the personality after death. They remain in the field of the culture's collective psychism for some time after death, their endurance depending upon their degree of integration during the person's life. As the principle of Unity waxes and dominates the principle of Multiplicity after the symbolic Sunset (physical death psychic remains are "experienced" (imperienced?) as subjective memories. As the cycle nears its symbolic Midnight, they gradually fade away, somewhat as leaves decay during winter. If the person has achieved an individualized condition during life – perhaps even establishing a degree of conscious attunement with the spiritual Quality – the "harvest" (positive and negative) of the life's individual experiences are "taken up" by the spiritual Quality. Successive harvests generate around the spiritual Quality what Rudhyar calls a **Soul Field**. The harvests and subjective memories the Soul Field contains become the karma of the next personality to become associated with it.

When the sub-subcycle of being constituted by an individual person reaches its phases of greatest subjectivity – its own relative Godhead state – the spiritual entity that sought to enter into at least partial relationship with the once-alive person is moved by compassion and compelled by karma to contact a new human being and to formulate the archetypal structure of a new dharma. From the point of view of the spiritual Quality, the new human being's task will be to perform this dharma, which will bring it into a closer relationship with the Soul Field than the previous personality achieved. The fulfillment of the new personality's dharma will involve the neutralization and "redemption" of the failures and the completion of the unfinished business of the old personality(ies). But the new human being is not the old human being reappeared. It is any human being ready to be born whose ancestry, biological characteristics, and natal circumstances could be the foundation for the performance of the new dharma. The biological characteristics also are conditioned by the Soul Field, for each of the three basic constituents of human being – the physical, the psychomental, and the spiritual – is "reflected" in each of the others.

Because the new dharma is determined by the karma of a once-living person, a cause-and-effect relationship links the deceased and the newborn. But to say that the former "reincarnates" in the latter is not accurate (for nothing actually "becomes flesh"). The new person succeeds to the dead one as holder of the same "office." Similarly, the president of a corporation "succeeds" his predecessor and inherits his karma – the problems he failed to solve – as well as the constructively functioning aspects of the organization he developed. The latter refer primarily to the level of mental development the previous personality achieved.

Thus, from Rudhyar's point of view, when a person says, "I was such-and-such person in a previous life," the person identifies with the dead person's karma (unfinished business and failures). What one ought to do instead is to try to understand, identify with, and perform one's present dharma, which, automatically, will neutralize this karma, move one forward in the evolutionary process, and attune one to the rising principle of Unity seeking to unite person (lesser whole) and spiritual Quality (aspect of the greater whole Anthropos or archetypal Man).

14. THE NATURE AND FUNCTION OF MIND

For Rudhyar, the general goal of human evolution in the present era is the development of an individualized, stable, and focused mind, able to deal with archetypal principles and processes, able to give meaning to all facets of experience in relation to one another. Such a mind, which Rudhyar calls the **mind of wholeness**, is the "alchemical vessel" or meeting place necessary to contain or hold the "divine marriage" between spiritual Quality and human personality.

In a broader sense, mind, for Rudhyar, is formed consciousness (consciousness in turn being inseparable from any kind of organized activity within a finite field). Mind operates at all levels as a universal formative principle. Form, however, inevitably divides existence into "inside" and "outside," self and not-self. As the formative principle, mind therefore deals with dualities. For Rudhyar, it is based on the interplay of two principles of being, Unity and Multiplicity (or Yin and Yang). This interplay must be cyclic and balanced (as long as we consider motion and activity as the foundation of being and the experience of change the inescapable reality of human existence). Therefore, in its highest (most inclusive) aspect, mind establishes and/or reveals the place and function of everything in relation to everything else.

Thus, in an overall philosophical sense, Rudhyar's conception of mind distinguishes his metaphysical outlook from others that can be considered ultimately dualistic. Much of the developing "new age" philosophical paradigm is based on a dualism (a reflection of the popularized Hindu view) between a supreme, transcendent, timeless, changeless condition (Reality with a capital R) and the illusion (*maya*) of the existential world. Such a dualism has been duplicated in the Platonic contrast between a realm of changeless archetypes and an existential world as unreal as flickering shadows projected on the wall of a cave; and in the Christian contrast between divine spirit and sinful human nature. But none of these dualisms is relieved or reconciled by anything "in between" – by a mediating, integrating factor convincingly or purposefully relating the two opposite conditions or realms. For Rudhyar, by contrast, these two realms, orders, or dimensions of being are always to some degree interrelated and interpenetrating – and mind is always the mediating, connecting factor.

During the period of the universal cycle of being between Midnight and Sunrise, mind balances the principles of Unity and Multiplicity by focusing into broadly-defined archetypal forms and formulas of relationship, the supreme compassion radiating from the Godhead state. Mind is thus involutionary and operates through various creative Hierarchies that religions call by various names (e.g., angels). Between Sunrise and Noon, the results of this cosmogenic mental activity serve as "guiding fields" for the development of cosmic material systems (galaxies, solar systems, planets) and for the evolution of biological orders, families, genera, and species. After the symbolic Noon, the coming of Natural Man, and his mental fecundation through the avataric process – which Rudhyar envisions as a projection of the Godhead's "vision-imaging" of a new universe into a "God seed" potential within human beings – mind develops in its generic, cultural, individual, and superindividual human modes.

At the biological level of human evolution, mind operates almost exclusively as the servant of instincts seeking to perpetuate life. It is a generic type of mind. As mind becomes sociocutural, it formulates words, language, religious symbols and myths, philosophical concepts, and a way of life. The function of this "mind of culture" is to give order and meaning to personal experience by referring it to the culture's collective frame of reference.[3]

As the separative ego-will isolates the human person from its cultural matrix, mind also individualizes and tries not to refer personal experience to a collective frame of reference. At first, the individualizing mind is the critical, analytical, discursive intellect, glorifying the principle of measurement and quantitative calculations at the expense of qualitative values. The abstract concepts of reason, logic, and natural "law" (an ambiguous term) replace the traditional symbols, myths, and taboos of the culture. As the intellect analyzes complex realities, it reduces them to "nothing but" component entities and patterns of relationship. Eventually it analyzes away the organic wholeness of integral entities and processes. Unguided by qualitative values, the intellec-

---

3 If spiritual teachers seeking to lead human beings to the Path of transformation have presented mind as something to be transcended — even as "the slayer of the Real" — it is because the forms mind builds have inertia. All sociocultural images and institutions resist change. When change is necessary, mind tends to resist it, to attempt to perpetuate unchanged the forms it had earlier engendered or revealed. The refusal to change when change is needed is always polarized by the catabolic activity of revolutionaries, political or spiritual: inertia and the rise of anarchy are two aspects of the same situation. Only by total nonattachment to any form, even if one inevitably must use forms of thinking and behavior, can one escape being caught up in the riptide of destruction dominating the last phases of a cycle, be it personal, cultural, or existential.

tual mind produces and wields a mighty technology which eventually runs amok; incalculable destruction and collective and individual suffering ensue.

Eventually, mind begins to build frames of reference which, though having an individual character, are conditioned by a realization of belonging to a metacultural, meta-individual whole. The "mind of wholeness" begins to operate and to supersede the analytical intellect. Instead of reducing complex realities to components, the mind of wholeness deduces the meaning of situations from the interaction of several interpenetrating levels of activity. It begins to see the "ground" out of which particularities differentiate and their inherent interrelatedness. In another sense, Rudhyar calls this kind of mental activity **"eonic consciousness"** (eon meaning a cycle of time). It is required to disentangle several complex, interpenetrating patterns or sets of relations, but it retains an understanding of the whole without reductionary analysis. It sees, both, the whole of a cycle of development and its constituting phases and entities and their complex interrelationships. It is with this kind of mind that Rudhyar examines human history and evolution as these processes proceed within the planetary life-field of the earth.

15. THE PLANETARY WHOLE AND THE PLACE AND FUNCTION OF HUMAN EVOLUTION WITHIN IT

On the one hand, for Rudhyar, the earth is the physical body of a planetary whole (now at times called *Gaia* or *Terra*) also operating and evolving at psychomental and spiritual levels. (Rudhyar was an early advocate of global organization as a sociopolitical reflection of this reality, and fifty years before the terms became fashionable, he spoke of "World Music" and "man's common humanity.") The character of the function which humanity performs within the total field of activity and consciousness of our planet might be evoked by comparing it to the work of the cerebrospinal nervous system and front-brain of a human being: mankind's function is thus to consciously formulate and give meaning to all the activities taking place on, in, or around the earth. This implies discovering the principles on which these activities are based and applying these principles to fulfill consciously determined purposes. The great problem of human evolution is, however, how and in relation to what frame of reference (what values) are these purposes to be determined?

On the other, the earth's biosphere is the planetary life-field in which the archetype Man develops its potentialities through the biological species Homo sapiens and through its development in culture-wholes giving rise to various types of persons and individuals. The activity, consciousness and evolution of humanity may be said to build the "psychosphere" and "noösphere" of our planet. The former (similar to the "astral plane" of popular occultism) refers to the psychism, collective and individual, of cultures and persons. The latter (a term devised by Teilhard de Chardin) refers to the activity and evolution of the rational aspect of the human mind. Above the psychosphere and noösphere, Rudhyar also conceives of a "pneumosphere" (spiritual sphere) being actualized by Pleroma beings according to the directions of still higher entities. The pneumosphere presumably envelops and contains the whole planet. (In all cases the term "sphere" may be confusing if one imagines geometrically concentric spheres separate from each other.)

16. RHYTHMS OF CULTURE AND CIVILIZATION

In line with the image of the earth's psychosphere and noösphere, another new and striking concept which Rudhyar presents deals with the relationship between what he calls the **process of civilization** and the many culture-wholes which are born, mature, and decay and which bring their cyclic harvests of symbols, institutions, and art forms to the gradual development of the earth's psychosphere. For Rudhyar, civilization is a planetary process bringing separate cultures into contact with one another, thereby creating a psychic-cultural ferment into which new potentialities of mind can be released. Hence the process of civilization refers to the development of the earth's noösphere.

In contrast to culture, which is local, exclusivistic, and anabolic (*Vishnu*), the process of civilization is global, inclusive, and (at least in its early stages and in relation to exclusivistic and inertial cultural structures) catabolic-transformative (*Shiva*). It operates by quantum leaps to release new mental energies, which fecundate and are absorbed by the psychomental substance of a culture-whole. The noetic function of the culture-whole is to embody the new mental quality. But cultural structures usually develop such strong inertia that they resist transformation and often pervert or actualize only partially the new mental possibilities. Thus, for Rudhyar, human cultures cyclically rise and fall and often fail to perform their functional roles, but the all-human process of civilization continues, nonetheless.

The process of civilization and the process of individualization are closely related. In one sense, they are two ways of interpreting the same process – civilization from a planetary perspective; individualization from the point of view of particular cultures and human beings. In another sense, the process of individualization is stimulated at first by the interaction of civilization and culture. When a culture-whole produces persons with minds sufficiently formed to respond to the principle of individuality, the process of civilization releases what Rudhyar calls a new mental **Tone** or vibration, and the process of individualization begins to affect both the culture and sensitive persons.

In all-human, planetary terms, the beginning of the process of individualization can be traced to what Greek tradition depicts as the Promethean gift, which Rudhyar refers to the beginning of the avataric process. In terms of our present cycle of human development, he relates this turning point to the beginning of what Hindu chronology calls *Kali Yuga* – the death of the avatar Krishna (3102 B.C.). As the process of civilization and mental individualization seems to operate in 500-year cycles (and in general according to what theosophists call vibration Five), the process of civilization reached another significant turning point about five 500-year cycles later – the sixth century B.C., the time of Pythagoras, Gautama Buddha, Lao Tze, and the last of the Zoroasters.[4] In the Greece of the sixth century B.C., the new mental vi-

---

4 Other significant turning points in the process of civilization in the interim are represented by the monotheistic reform of Akhnaton in Egypt and the period of the Upanishads in India – both in the second millennium B.C. During the latter, the concept of atman (the spiritual identity of a human being) was developed and its identity with the universal Brahman was proclaimed; Akhnaton announced the correspondence of the Self within man with the Sun-disc.

bration took form in the glorification of reason (*nous*) and the principle of measurement. In India, the Buddha taught the transcendence of the caste system and the power of the human mind to detach itself from the forms of existence that engendered *dukka*.

Five 500-year cycles later brings us to the beginning of our own tumultuous century, which so far has seen the intermingling and destruction (or at least destructuring) of all the world's cultures through two world wars and the technological developments that allowed human beings to realize the interchangeability of matter and energy and to see the wholeness of the earth-globe from space. The latter especially has fecundated the human mind and imagination with new possibilities, many of which are concentrated in the terms "transformation" and "transpersonal."

17. THE PROCESS OF TRANSFORMATION

The process of transformation requires individualization as a foundation. It is the process whereby separative, self-centered individuals – often still bound to, or rebelling against, their natal cultures, are mostly in a state of disarray and disintegration; their myths, symbols, and images having lost the power to wholesomely integrate the collective psychism and their way of life breaking down – reorient their minds and feeling-natures toward an awareness of the primacy of the whole and consecrate themselves to the service of humanity. This does not, however, mean that they must "save the world" or "do good" for others; it means that they must, first, consciously attune themselves to the performance of their own dharma, on behalf of the greater whole, archetypal Man, which is trying to contact them.

While the process of transformation has immense psychological implications, for Rudhyar it is essentially an occult process often called **"the Path."** It is supported by well-organized (but historically ignored, materialized, or psychologized) spiritual and metaphysical forces. Its goal is the transindividual level – Pleroma consciousness.

18. TRANSPERSONAL ACTIVITY

While psychologists and philosophers now use the term "transpersonal" to refer to experiences or states of consciousness **beyond** the usual human range, Rudhyar has always used it to refer to the deliberate, focused, and functional action of spiritual forces **through** a human being. He probably was the first to use the term in English, in 1930 in an article published in the magazine "The Glass Hive":

> Instead of impersonal, let us use another word more telling – transpersonal. A personal behavior (or feeling or thought) is one rooted in the substance and conditioned form of the personality. A transpersonal behavior is one starting from the universal, unconditioned self in Man and using the personality merely as an instrument.

Hence the source of transpersonal activity may be interpreted as being the spiritual Quality seeking to contact an individual person; the archetype Man seeking to reveal a particular aspect of anthropic potentiality to humanity or to a particular culture-whole through him or her; or the Pleroma seeking to guide, test, or assist an individual or group of individuals treading the Path of transformation. Holarchically speaking, transpersonal activity represents a focusing of power from a greater through a lesser whole.

For Rudhyar, however, transpersonal activity is not mere "channeling" or passive mediumship. For him, the latter operates primarily at the level of psychism (collective or individual), while the former must be focused by an individual's well-formed mind if it is to be truly transpersonal. Symbolically speaking, the mind of the true transpersonal agent operates not merely as a pane of glass allowing the passage of diffuse light, but as a clear lens bringing light to a sharp focus. For while light passing through a window does so relatively unchanged, light focused through a lens can ignite material at the focal point. Thus is "light" (spirit) concentrated into "heat" (symbol of increasing speed of motion and change) and eventually into the incandescence of the Pleroma state.

19. THE PROCESS OF DECONDITIONING AND RENEWAL

When asked how he feels or what he thinks about prospects ahead for mankind, Rudhyar often replies that he is pessimistic in the short run and optimistic in the long run. He was among the first to realize that, in this century, humanity faces a major crisis of transformation on all fronts, but he has no doubt that sooner or later, in one place, century, or culture or another, humanity will meet the challenge – but the quality of the transformation and the number of human beings affected positively by it could be greatly diminished, depending on how humanity collectively responds to circumstances in the next decades.

Rudhyar's overall view of human cultural development can be expressed in dialectical terms: thesis, antithesis, synthesis. Tribal society – and all it implies in terms of psychic unanimity and a sense of the sacred – represents the thesis. Western individualism and the dominance of a highly intellectualized, abstract mind producing and greedily wielding a destructive technology represent the antithesis. The synthesis is yet ahead and should incorporate the basic values of the two preceding stages – but within a more inclusive (planetary...and beyond) frame of reference and within a spirit-oriented consciousness.

For Rudhyar, much that is progressive in society today – for example, attempts to integrate Eastern and Western culture and religion, science and spirituality – represent stages in a necessary process of **deconditioning** ("deculturalization" or "dis-Europeanization"). But deconditioning is only a prelude to transformation and rebirth: it is not itself renewal. Rudhyar's fervent hope is that new symbols and images – in philosophy, psychology, social organization, and the arts – will evoke the development of a new mentality: the mind of wholeness, the mind that "sees" rather than cogitates and argues pro and con, the mind of the Sage that allows all life, events, and relationships to pass through its structured openness and in so passing acquire **meaning**. This "new" mentality would also operate as the "cosmogenic mind" able to see the potentialities of, and project order upon, the apparent chaos of present day social and cultural existence.

III.

RUDHYAR'S INTEGRATION OF EXPERIENCE AND CONCEPTS

1. THE ARTS

Rudhyar's activities in the arts always have been a spontaneous, very personal – yet transpersonal – expression, unburdened by prolonged technical training or conditioning; and they unselfconsciously exemplify his philosophy and demonstrate his overall attitude to life.

For Rudhyar, art – its production and experience – has a different function at different stages of cultural development. The six levels of art-activity that follow can be adapted to apply to all the arts (poetry, literature, drama, music, painting, and sculpture) and correspond to stages in the development of a culture-whole:

1. Art as release of power through magical forms

Magical, or so-called primitive, art has as its aim the "purposeful release of focalized power through an effective form in answer to a need." (Quoting Rudhyar from memory from *Art as Release of Power*.) Primitive art is essentially a means for magical action: magical objects are functional (intended to kill, tame, control, evoke animals or natural or elemental forces); they do not aim to be beautiful according to esthetic standards, for culture has not yet developed these.

2. Art as decorative enhancement of value

Not essentially different from magical, but meant to display the skill of the maker and/or the wealth and taste of the owner; bridge between purely magical-functional art and esthetic art.

3. Art as esthetic enjoyment of cultural forms

Art expressing the classical period of a culture; appreciated according to culturally defined esthetic values, the main function of which is to reveal the principles of order and proportion that give members of the culture a sense of peace, security, or exaltation. Eventually leads to "art for art's sake."

4. Art as personal expression

The art of a culture's romantic period; art as autobiography expressing and glorifying the sufferings and, more rarely, the triumphs of the individual. Romanticism leads to Expressionism, surrealism, and the many varieties of avant-garde art, the main function of which is to decondition the consciousness of both artists and art lovers from conditioned cultural values and taboos.

5. *Art as catharsis and mantra of rebirth*

The art of a culture in crisis; artists act as agents for catabolic action, eventually destroying what is left of the disintegrating collective psychism. Eventually leads to reactionary movements – neoprimitivism, neoscholasticism, neoclassicism.

6. *Art as [transpersonal] Hierophany*

Art as a transcultural factor (working through culture but not of culture). This type of art could be called "transcrete" art – that is, meaning "grows through" or is revealed through its forms. Rudhyar also calls it mythopoetic seed art, which projects into the planetary psyche new images to galvanize a new consciousness and new culture.

A. POETRY

The following is quoted from the Foreword of Rudhyar's *Of Vibrancy and Peace* (1967), an anthology of poems from 1916 to 1962:

> My poetry was not written with the view of conforming to a literary tradition and to fit into esthetically appreciable forms. It is the quite spontaneous expression of my inner life; it was written in most cases of time of great stress, of challenging, perhaps devastating emotional and/or spiritual experiences. It was meant to

express and to communicate the fervor and intensity of what psychologists now often call "peak experiences."

The poet [in the original sense of the Greek term] is he who acts as 'mover and shaker'of souls, stimulating his audience to feel more deeply, more totally than their ordinary lives allow...He opens new vistas, new levels of vision, new depths of relationship – of love, pain or ecstasy. He presents new images, connects in new ways until then distant facts of human experience. He evokes new dawns, expands man's consciousness and man's eagerness to reach into the unknown.

The following is paraphrased (interspersed with quotations) from Rudhyar's unpublished autobiography (1980):

Poetry means something different in each period of a culture. "In the early stages of a culture's development, poetry always has an essentially magical, epic or sacred character. Mantras and magical or theurgic formulas are the initial sources of what later becomes epic and religious poetry." At first "poetry and music are hardly distinguishable." The poet is the bard who intones poems (linked with dramatic gestures) narrating the culture's myths and legends. The poet thus builds and later helps to maintain the collective psychism of the culture.

Only when a culture reaches the Romantic phase of its development does the poet act as an individual for whom poetry is a means for 'self-expression.' Instead of narrating the lives and deeds of legendary heroes, the poet becomes the central figure whose life, passions, sufferings and joys poetry reveal. This self-expression, however, also means 'self-revelation – a veiling, in symbolic forms, what the poet has either experienced or is unable to act out.

"The majority of my poems have exteriorized, in symbolic words and images, what in me had been unable to find manifestation in concrete everyday living and actual interpersonal relationships. They reveal potentialities whose actualization was but too often made impossible by the outer circumstances and/or inner pressures of my life. They reveal a level of my inner life which could be made concrete only in symbols rather than in actual physical happenings."

"The reason for this is far more basic than one initially might think...A great many human beings...succeed relatively well in actualizing their birth potential, because the latter fits rather smoothly into the collective framework of family, culture, and religion...In times of transition between historical cycles and under special circumstances...other individuals are born with a far vaster potential of being than can be actualized at the time and in the place they were born. We say that they are 'ahead of their times,' pioneers of a future type of consciousness and interpersonal relationship. The result is that they face the near-impossibility of actualizing their inner potential – their dharma, their essential being. As they are so often unable to resolve the tension of the polar forces within their personality in terms of actual and fulfilling experiences, they are driven by an inner power to produce a liberating solution at the symbolic level of literature or of another artistic or concept-formulating activity."

"A culture, having reached the last stage of its development, **needs** such individuals. In a very real sense, their frustrations and apparent failures at the level of actual sociocultural happenings are the very roots of their spiritual successes as transformative agents. Through their attempts to provide concrete existential solutions to their actually insoluble inner tensions...they create poems, music, paintings, etc., giving symbolic forms to future sociocultural processes. They thus release seeds of futurity – archetypes that eventually will become the paradigms of a new society and/or culture."

B. LITERATURE

Rudhyar's two main novels are *Rania* (written in 1929, but not published until 1974) and *Return from No Return* (written in 1953, but not published until 1973):

Rania is the "epic narrative" of a woman's life, from "passionate spring" through "spiritual flowering" and the "sacrifice of the seed" (quoted are the subtitles of the book's three sections or "movements").

Rania was written during three intense weeks in Chicago in January 1929. It incorporates experiences Rudhyar had in Carmel and in Hollywood's motion picture world – he had been an extra and bit player in silent and early sound pictures. The plot is centered around magnified features in which are telescoped and integrated features of people he had known; as he wrote it he intuited that he was on the threshold of a new period of his life – he met the woman who became his first wife shortly thereafter.

These personal experiences and memories are magnified into archetypal images operating within an equally archetypal plot: the inter- and intrapersonal struggle between forces of light and darkness, resolved by the redeeming sacrifice. To give the narrative an epic quality, Rudhyar used the device of poetic stanzas with repeated lines; the stanzas become longer as the action develops, gradually coalescing into prose paragraphs – but the poetic device returns at the end.

Return from No Return is a metaphysical science fiction novel. It is set in the twenty-second century, on earth and in intergalactic and "interincarnational" space. It weaves together the drama of a global crisis, an intense story of transpersonal love, and a presentation of an esoteric concept of space and the possibility of integral existence beyond physical death.

Common to both novels are heroic, spiritually oriented female protagonists whose spiritual triumphs and failures are portrayed sympathetically, and the redemptive power of unselfish, transpersonal love. Many young women have especially identified with Rania, and a professor of literature once commented that it read as if it had been written by C. G. Jung, M. Esther Harding, and D. H. Lawrence – then rewritten by Madame Blavatsky!

Attempts have been made to make feature films of both novels. *Return from No Return* was especially considered after the phenomenal success of "Star Wars," but as there seemed no possibility of making a commercially viable film without losing the work's essential qualities, the project was stopped.

C. MUSIC

There was absolutely no musical (or artistic or literary) precedence for Rudhyar's creativity in his family background – a relatively well-to-do middle class Parisian family. He received early lessons in piano and solfege with distaste, and they soon were stopped due to life-threatening illness. But playing piano, reading orchestral scores, improvising, and composing came naturally to him (perhaps bequeathed by a "predecessor" in relation to the Soul Field). His first experiences of orchestral music fascinated him.

He intuited that Debussy and his music were representative of the closing ("autumnal") phase of European culture. Out of this intuition came his first book, "Claude Debussy and the Cycle of Musical Civilization," which he wrote at the age of sixteen. A revised version of the first part of it – sans philosophy – was published by Durand, Debussy's publisher, along with Rudhyar's first three piano compositions (1916).

Music provided the means for Rudhyar to come to America – a performance of an ultramodern type of multimedia presentation (dance, music, light, color, incense), for which Rudhyar had written the orchestral music, was given at the Metropolitan Opera in New York in April 1917. But it was too far ahead of its time to arouse appreciation and understanding, and it was eclipsed by America's entrance into World War I, which was announced the very night the performance was given.

Rudhyar's music is composed at the piano, unintellectually and without attention to preconceived forms, patterns of development, or rules. It is "essentially the exteriorization of inner experiences and states of consciousness and feelings. It is subjective rather than the development of objective and intellectually analyzable patterns conditioned by our culture."

Its "only purpose – if one can really speak of 'purpose' in such a context – has been to stir people, to remove emotional and traditional obstacles, vanquish psychic stagnation and set psyches, souls or minds free to be fully, eagerly, intensely themselves, regardless of what parents and society forced them to be."

Rudhyar stresses that in composing music he is not, like so many other composers past and present, fashioning or contriving musical "objects." For him, music is and should be the exteriorization in tone of an inner life – the flow of life (or in Ira Progoff's sense, the psyche) itself.

In his writings on music, Rudhyar has dealt with, among others, the following themes:

1) Primordially, Sound (with a capital S) is an inaudible *anahata* in Sanskrit, creative, metaphysical force that precipitates (as it were) the divine Idea of a universe into objective material manifestation. It has essentially a "descending" movement to which matter resonates by producing ascending progressions of audible sounds (the harmonic series of fundamental and overtones modified by the timbre or characteristic tone-quality of particular instruments or relating bodies).

2) Music, on the other hand, is an art: the organization of sounds a particular culture develops. What is acceptable in music therefore varies from culture to culture and from stage to stage in a culture's development.

   "The historical development of music follows, and can be understood only in terms of, the unfoldment of the human mind, which builds the systems of organization giving stable structures to the sounds the people of any culture need for communicating their collective needs and responses."

Thus, for Rudhyar, music is a culturally-conditioned language for communication at the psychic level – the level of the culture's collective psychism. Long before Eastern music was acceptable to Western musicians and musicologists – they called it "barbaric noise" – Rudhyar stressed that Oriental music was as valid and serves the same function in Eastern cultures as Western music does in Western cultures.

The question of whether music can ever be a truly universal language is, for Rudhyar, an open question, depending upon how cultures and minds respond to the new mental vibrations of the all-human process of civilization.

3) Notes versus Tones: For Rudhyar, the tonality-dominated notes of Western music are abstract entities having musical meaning only in relation to one another; as they can be transposed or played on a variety of instruments without altering their musical meaning, they do not refer to the experience of actual, particular sounds. Moreover, in the West music resides more in the written score than in the actual experience of hearing it. Western musical works are "objects" whose formal structures and developmental patterns are to be appreciated more by the eyes and intellect than by the ears and psyche.

4) In early tribal societies, on the other hand, tones were used for magical purposes – that is, for the transmission of will and the subjugation of biological energies. Notes and intervals were not "spatialized" by being written down but were dealt with instinctively and psychically.

5) In the early magical use of tones, sonic progressions (what we call "scales") were felt to descend (that is, to proceed naturally from high to low pitch). This use of tones by early peoples reflected the "descent" of inaudible Sound in the cosmogenic process. The great evolutionary change in human consciousness that occurred in the fifth and sixth centuries B.C. had its parallel in music in the reversal of musical consciousness: the "natural" way of producing and hearing sound switched from being descending to being ascending. This change probably was implied in, and spread by, the Pythagorean use of the monochord as a didactic instrument. In using the monochord, Pythagoras was attempting to demonstrate the operation of impersonal, metabiological principles of number and form as the foundation of existence. His teachings and reform in Greece paralleled the activity of his contemporary, Gautama Buddha, in India – and both were manifestations of the release of a new mental vibration spurring the process of individualization.

6) Western tonality developed on the foundation of the measurement of exact frequencies of sounds and intervals, a written musical notation "spatializing" music, and polyphony – all of which are products of the kind of intellectual mind developing in the West since the sixth century B.C. Polyphony paralleled the acceleration of the process of individualization in European culture: whereas tribal peoples express their psychic unanimity by singing "as of one voice," the members of a soci-

ety affected by the process of individualization feel moved to express their individual differences in multiple melodic lines. Tonality became necessary to integrate this centrifugal kind of music.

7) Tonality is the musical equivalent of the autocratic rule of the king (the tonic), his prime minister (the dominant), and a bureaucracy that measures and enforces relationships within the whole. In a pluralistic European culture, the music of which consists of abstract notes, it substitutes for the psychic power of integration what once was inherent in sequences of communicative tones.

8) The tonality-system had to be transcended sooner or later, and late Romantic works (for example, the late works of Franz Liszt) pushed the structure to its limits. The process of transcending tonality in music parallels what Rudhyar calls the "deculturalization" and "dis-Europeanization" of Western consciousness.

Four composers of the late nineteenth and early twentieth century were central to this process: Scriabin, by trying to pour a mystical consciousness into old forms and instruments; Satie, by spoofing musical conventions and thereby becoming the precursor of Dadaism and the anarchic type of avant-garde; Stravinsky, by stunning the European aristocracy with the neoprimitivism of his "Rite of Spring," thereby opening the possibility of a renewed sacro-magical use of sound (but, frightened by the primal power of what he had released, he sought refuge in retreat – neoclassicism); and Schoenberg, by abandoning tonality altogeth-

er (but he replaced it with other rigid intellectual rules that were, for Rudhyar, "like substituting totalitarianism to the divine right of kings.")
9) Of the various trends of avant-garde music developed since World War I, Rudhyar believes that most are a continuation of the cathartic, catabolic process of deconditioning. But, for him, deconditioning and severance from the past are necessary before any significant rebirth or transformation can occur, and he feels the same way about most trends in contemporary society.

The current "minimalism" in avant-garde music, especially "meditation music" composed of simple, highly repetitive statements simulating ancient magical practices – having been strongly influenced by its composers' experiences of psychedelic drugs and Eastern philosophies and practices (often highly modified for Western consumption), also represents mainly a deconditioning process.

Since young composers opposed to the materialism of Western culture have to face the difficult problem of having their works performed by highly paid professional musicians, they often resort to electronic instruments – products of the very technological mentality they decry – the actual tones of which sound, to Rudhyar, hollow and devoid of a human, expressive, or ensouling quality. On the other hand, while the actual tones produced by some composer musicians working with acoustically resonant instruments (gongs or bells, for example) have this ensouling quality and beauty, the organization of sounds into music lacks cohesion and inspiration and often banalizes the tones used.

10) For Rudhyar, any truly significant rebirth or transformation in music must integrate within a broader, more inclusive frame of reference and organized consciousness values of both non-Western, sacromagical music and features of the Western mental approach based on proportion and form. Needed for the development of a new musical consciousness and thus a truly new music are:
    - A new sense of musical space paralleling a new philosophical and metaphysical understanding of space: space as fulness of being rather than space as an empty container in which unrelated material entities act and react according to "natural laws";
    - A renewed sense of the sacred in sound;
    - A new sense of "holistic resonance" of actual tones;
    - A new sense of organization in music.
11) Consonant versus Dissonant Harmony: Since 1925 Rudhyar has spoken "of the difference between consonant and dissonant harmony, a distinction which applies not only to music, but to all types of relationships. I spoke therefore of the Consonant and Dissonant Orders of relationships."

"While the Consonant Order finds its unifying principle in a unity of origin (the fundamental tone, No. 1), the Dissonant Order experiences unity (or rather, **multi-unity**) in the cooperative association of equal entities, each with a different character. In terms of social organization, the

Consonant Order manifests as the tribal order, spiritually, if not biologically, rooted in a common Great Ancestor who lived in a more or less mythical **past**; the Dissonant Order refers to the true democratic [or companionate] order in which individuals, who are basically different and equal, come together in order to work out a common purpose to be fulfilled in the **future**.

"A typically consonant, tonal music is ruled by the tonic and the dominant, just as ancient monarchies were ruled by the king and the prime minister...Everything in the realm theoretically belonged to the king, and all developments followed a formalistic principle embodying variations on a root unity. The emphasis was on looking back to the original one."

"The dissonant approach to music, to society, and to human existence in general moves in an opposite direction. Unity is not given, it is to be made in the consciousness of the auditors. Life and music constitute, from this point of view, a problem of integration. One can still speak of a unity of origin in a metaphysical or occult sense, but this dissonant approach is existential in that it deals with what exists now – that is, with separate individuals engaged today in a vast process of global harmonization, individuals seeking to organize their differences, so as to reach a state of all-inclusive integration, a state of plenitude."

Recently, Rudhyar has begun to think about substituting the term "transsonant" for dissonant, to evoke the possibility of a dissonant, highly resonant sound acting as a vehicle **through which** inspiriting meaning could be transmitted. More than new developments in composition, performance technique, or instruments, however, a transsonant use of sound would depend primarily on the level of consciousness of the composer-performer and the hearers.

12) While Rudhyar has written orchestral and chamber music, he has composed mainly for the piano, pioneering a technique which he calls "orchestral pianism," in which the total resonance of tone produced is more significant than separate notes and formal articulation. For him, the basic sonic material produced by a piano comes from the "holistic resonance" of its entire sounding board rather than from the separate vibrations of its strings. Moreover, for him, the "physical world of human experience is not unlike an immense sounding board; and the sounding board of a piano is the best illustration or symbol afforded by Western music, because the seven octaves of the piano symbolize the normal extension of our practically usable musical space."

For Rudhyar, it is significant that one person at the piano can "directly manipulate the...whole musical space to which human beings can respond," and can "fecundate" it with his or her creative will and individualized psychism. This act of fecundation parallels in human experience the descending activity of cosmogenic (inaudible) Sound: the creative will and emotions of the performer impact the keys of the piano, and the resonant material of the piano's sounding board produces audible tone carrying the "message" of the creative intent.

D. PAINTING

Rudhyar began to paint in Santa Fe, New Mexico, in 1938 (age 43). At the time, his musical activity had been completely stopped (mostly because he "strenuously opposed" neoclassicism in music, and a group of influential neoclassical musicians controlled the "musical scene" in terms of performances, grants, and commissions – and because the Great Depression and the graduated income tax discouraged wealthy patrons from supporting independent creative artists as they previously had). He found himself among painters, participating in discussions concerning art, the attitude of the artist, the value of technique, the relation of esthetics to spirituality, and so on. He felt he should demonstrate in practice some of the points he had made in these discussions. The following is quoted from his unpublished autobiography (1980):

> "One of them was my belief that a truly creative artist should be able to create significant and original – even if not technically masterful – works in **any** art… A period of familiarization with the materials used in the new art, and particularly of establishing reliable muscular connections through the nerves between the brain centers and the hand used in the creative process, would obviously be needed; yet any material can be 'inspirited' by the same creative power acting **through** the creative person and his or her physical body…
>
> "In cultural periods where a 'style' – a collective social factor – is a more or less inescapable reality, and any budding artist must become subservient to its dictates, which he dare alter somewhat only after he is estab-

lished and even then at his risk and peril, the situation is different. But – and this is the essential theme of my life-work and destiny – we are **not** in such a period of collective style today, or rather we should not be… We are in a 'seed period' in which the supreme function of any really creative person is to be a 'prophet,' a Promethean spirit, not merely modifying the old Tradition a little, but starting from an almost totally different basis of consciousness. The artist should be reborn in a new world of feeling, thinking, seeing, and hearing. What is demanded of art (and of philosophy and religion as well) is a new perspective on existence. The creative person should become a lens through which new symbols can condense, focusing a new sense of reality in concrete form. A new 'language' of forms and values thus can, should, and must be built…

"Strictly representational painting…reduces to two-dimensional space the physical reality of objects and persons our senses and mind interpret as three-dimensional, using the principle of perspective and the direction of light and shadows to produce the appearance of concreteness. But as Kandinsky…well understood, this appearance is only an 'illusion.' Thus, he said, representative paintings are in fact 'abstractions.' This is why he spoke of his non-representative painting as 'concrete art.' Such an art does not try to mirror on a flat surface what we experience normally in depth; concrete art simply produces concrete objects – paintings – which do not pretend to exist in anything other than two-dimensional space. They are truly creations, not merely interpretations.

"I soon became aware that the proper term to characterize my paintings was **transcrete** art, because they were not objects having meaning in themselves as much as forms translucent to the light of meaning. The word 'transcrete' is made of the Latin roots *trans* (through) and *crescere* (to grow). Meaning grows out of the transcrete form as a plant grows out of a seed. The term, diaphanous, could also be used, because the forms in my paintings are (or at least purport to be) revelations of a transcendent quality or archetype of being…

"The problem one faces in dealing with such an approach to creativity deals with the part which the mind and the personal ego of the artist plays in the creative process: Does the process begin with the artist's emotional reactions or desire for success, etc., or does it have its source at a deeper level transcending the personality? As creative activity deals with materials (brushes, paint, pencils, canvas, paper, etc.), the ego, having learned to deal with earth-materials and everyday circumstances – for this is its function – is needed to watch over and guide what is taking place between the hand and the materials. It also should have acquired certain consciously accepted principles of balance and cyclic structure which can…be guiding elements which, for example, may suggest when the development can be best concluded or how a certain emphasis could be made stronger by a compensating factor. But the ego should not **cause** the creative act to happen. If it starts the process – for one reason or another (and the ego has so many 'reasons' and often rationalizations!) – it may find itself eventually pushed aside and 'the real thing' beginning, entirely changing what it thought it had started. If the ego is not pushed aside, then this 'real thing' does not happen. The artwork may still be 'interesting,' but it lacks the **power of evocation** which is, to me, the essential requisite of true art."

[This power of evocation means that art must] "release in concrete and significant forms **the power that creates a culture**. It must project the 'prime symbols,' new vistas in understanding, a new sense of reality…a new vision of humanity's essential purposes. By 'significant forms,' therefore, I do not mean form as the solution of merely esthetical problems of organization of lines, patterns, colors, spaces. Form as an end in itself, and art for art's sake, refers to the realm of **decorative** art. To me, great and vital art, instead, is always **evocative** art."

"It does not seem important to me that people seeing my paintings should know what **I** felt, why and how **I** produced them. The essential thing is the viewers' response – what the paintings **do to them**, what arises in them as a result of their seeing the paintings, of their **relationship** with the painting. It is, I believe, a matter of relationship: 'something' in the painting meets 'something' in the spectator; what is important is the character and quality of this meeting.

"At least thirty-five years after I painted my most significant paintings, a new generation has responded warmly to my writings and music. But these same youths, while impressed, are often puzzled by my paintings.] I am repeatedly asked what the paintings mean, how the evident symbols in them are to be understood. The onlooker's mind today is often conversant with the precise, intellectually formulated and listed meanings given to specific symbols, either in Freudian or Jungian psychologies or in the clearly catalogued teachings of Asian, Kabbalistic or Sufi philosophies...

"When facing my paintings, a person's reaction is often that I must have used such geometrical or biologically suggestive symbols deliberately, knowing exactly why I used them. People frequently are shocked when I tell them that I did not have precise intentions and did not think of traditional meanings. Then they often want to speak of 'the unconscious' – my personal unconscious or the 'collective unconscious' with its Jungian archetypes – guiding my hand in a psychological sense. If the onlookers are...interested in occult symbolism or metaphysics, the interpretations they give in most instances seem strange to me. [They] seem not to see what in several of my paintings or drawings is rather clearly an archetypal structure based on the interplay of forces within the human body. This has been [especially] the case [with] "Creative Man," "Meditation on Power"...or "Avatar."

"In my large pencil drawing, "The Alchemist," centers and currents of energy are clearly evoked by curving lines and geometrical forms. But persons familiar with the places and symbolical shapes of the chakras in the Tantric occultism of India and Tibet have been puzzled by what I have drawn, because the lines and forms are not in their traditional places in what is clearly a person in profile sitting with a raised knee and holding an alchemical lamp. They are even more puzzled if I tell them that they should forget the traditional system of knowledge and simply try **to experience** the drawing and allow it to speak to them and communicate a 'mystery' which perhaps transcends or has meaning besides the traditional knowledge."

2. ASTROLOGY

Any person having the possibility of working, consciously or unconsciously, at whatever level, as an agent for sociocultural transformation has somehow to establish an effective relation with some developing trend in the society whose collective or group consciousness is to be transformed. While the fields of music and the philosophy of culture were the first in which Rudhyar demonstrated his transformative vision, when he came to America (November 1916 to New York, January 1920 to Los Angeles), these fields were most undeveloped, and the response to his revolutionary ideas was minimal. After 1932, Rudhyar's activity in the field of astrology, which barely existed in America at the time, became the means to establish the necessary contact with a potentially large American public. This contact was made possible by Paul Clancy, who offered to Rudhyar the pages of his new magazine *American Astrology*, which soon became successful. Clancy gave Rudhyar carte blanche to use the magazine as a channel for his astrological reform along psychospiritual and philosophical lines.

Rudhyar had learned the principles and techniques of traditional astrology in 1920-21, at the headquarters of the Theosophical Society at Krotona. He had come there to write scenic music for the *Pilgrimage Play* depicting the life of Christ, and it was there that he came in close contact with theosophical and, in general, occult doctrines. The books on astrology he read were mostly by Alan Leo and Sepharial, both of whom were theosophists trying to revive classical European astrology in England, and by the Rosicrucian, Max Heindl.

In 1931, the mimeographed courses on astrology written by the philosopher-occultist Marc Edmund Jones for his small experimental group, the Sabian Assembly (of which Rudhyar was never a member), made him aware of new possibilities for astrology. In 1932 and 1933, his reading of the first translated books of the psychologist C. G. Jung of *Holism and Evolution* by the philosopher-statesman Jan Smuts, and works on the new Einsteinian physics, sparked in his mind the idea of integrating astrology and depth psychology in terms of the holistic approach emerging in philosophy and atomic physics. In relation to his theosophical and metaphysical studies, he realized that astrology could serve as a link between the cosmic and the psychological. In relation to depth psychology, which dealt with the **contents** of the psyche, a reformulated astrology could reveal the basic **structure** of a person's personality and life.

The Great Depression (which made it impossible for him to continue giving lecture-recitals at the homes of patrons of the arts) and the practical responsibilities of his marriage in 1930 made Paul Clancy's offer to publish monthly articles in *American Astrology* still more important. Alice Bailey's subsequent offer to publish Rudhyar's first large treatise on astrology, *The Astrology of Personality* (1936), and *New Mansions for New Men* (1938) added even more weight to his new enterprise.

During the next forty years, Rudhyar published several articles each month, not only in *American Astrology*, where he filled a section entitled "Psychological Astrology," but also (after 1939) in *Horoscope, World Astrology, Current Astrology, The Astrologer*, and others. Some of these articles were published under the pseudonyms Francis J. Ramsay and Daniel Morison, so as to avoid having too many articles by the same author in one issue of a magazine. In all, Rudhyar wrote about a thousand articles, of which an estimated quarter of a trillion copies were printed and circulated.

The basic ideas Rudhyar outlined in his articles eventually were incorporated into more than twenty books on astrology, many of which have been translated, some into multiple languages. Almost single handedly, he reformulated astrology in the twentieth century. While many ideas he was the first to formulate have now become integral to modern astrological thinking, many also have become materialized, "pop-psychologized," or banalized by being only partly understood or taken out of context, and many recent students of astrology may be unaware of their origin. Nevertheless, the popularity of his astrological ideas continues to grow in America and abroad – as well as recognition of him as a philosopher with a new cosmic, as well as psychological, vision.

Technical and specific interpretive matters aside, Rudhyar has stressed the following themes, among others, in astrology:

1) The function of astrology in all ancient cultures has been to answer man's most basic need – the need to feel secure by seeing order in existence. Or, one could also say, that the perception of celestial order confirms man's innate belief that there **is** order in existence. In either case, the perception of celestial order (astrology) has been the basis of all culture, religion, and science.

2) Why the revival of interest in astrology: The two basic frames of reference for order and security in Euro-American culture are science and religion. Reacting against and compensating for centuries of religious dogmatism, the modern mind has become, both, pervaded by glamor and illusions concerning science and disillusioned with it. This is because of the spectacular success of science and its technology's dismal failure to make life more secure. "No wonder then that distraught members of an equally chaotic society increasingly turn to ancient concepts of order and security."

3) Rudhyar does not, however, see the revival of interest in astrology as **only** a return to ancient concepts. He sees "a **transformed** astrology as a door into a future realm of understanding order and feeling secure. He writes, "My ultimate aim in reformulating astrology has not been to help people using or studying astrology feel secure by **avoiding** the unpredictable and traumatic. It has been to transform the search for a static kind of security-by-avoidance into a search for a dynamic kind of security that can be achieved only through **understanding** the place and meaning of the cathartic and transformative in human life."

4) There is no one thing called Astrology (with a capital A). There are, and have been, many astrologies, each representing the kind of order a particular culture sees in celestial motions, the kind of relationship the culture formulates between heaven and earth.

The kind of order and security astrology can provide today is **symbolic** and **holarchic**. Rudhyar does not rely upon theories of planetary "influences" or "energies" to justify astrology but believes that our culture's perceptions of celestial order – the solar system – is for us a symbol of the greater whole in which we "live, move, and have our being."

Signs of the zodiac, planets, aspects (that is, angular relationships between planets), houses of the horoscope, and so on are all symbols derived from our culture's astronomical facts of celestial motions; they symbolize basic principles and functional activities that operate everywhere according to parallel or corresponding rhythms – in the sky, in human collectivities, in the lives of individual persons. In other words, whatever has ordered and organized the solar system, and the motions of the planets also orders processes of existence on earth.

For Rudhyar, astrology is a **symbolic language** wherein a part (or lesser whole – a person) can read the "message" of the greater whole writ large.

5) For a particular person, this celestial message is symbolized by his or her horoscope – a map of the celestial situation at the exact time, from the perspective of the particular place, of the newborn's first breath. This first breath symbolically and existentially unites the newborn with the whole biosphere – air being the element that, circulating rapidly around the whole planet, is breathed by all living creatures.

The birth chart is essentially a symbol of the **need** of the greater whole in potential answer to which one's birth occurred. It is one's "celestial name," one's dharma or truth-of-being, what one is born **for**. Rudhyar's approach to astrology is thus **purposive** rather than merely **descriptive**: it aims at helping human beings fulfill the purpose for which they were born. Nothing in a birth chart, transits, or progressions (actual and symbolic celestial motions after birth) is in itself "good" or "bad," "fortunate" or "unfortunate." Everything astrological and existential is what it is because it **needs** to be that way.

Astrological symbols reveal structural, not existential knowledge. Progressions and transits are like clocks and calendars: they symbolize the passage of time and mark its structural divisions or turning points; they do not make things happen. In relation to actual events and periods of life, they symbolize particular functional activities or life-themes and thus reveal ("re-veil") the **meaning** of the event or period. They do not indicate precisely what will happen.

6) Rudhyar was likely the first to stress the astrologer's psychological responsibility to the client: the astrologer should function neither as oracle nor judge, but as a "consultant" to the' client, bearing in mind the psychological implications of predictions ("good" or "bad") or pronouncements. The astrologer's main aim should be to help the client **understand** the meaning of his or her situation, of what has happened in the past, and how all experiences and events can be seen as phases of a process from birth to death.

7) In order to clarify his approach and differentiate it from others, Rudhyar has called it by various names:

Harmonic astrology was used mainly in the 1930s and '40s. The term was meant to show that astrology could reveal the "harmony of the whole person." It saw the birth chart as a formula for integrating the various aspects and functions of the personality for maximum intensity and fulfillment in living.

Person-centered astrology – This term was used in the late 1960s in contrast to "event-oriented" astrology. It was meant to evoke the idea that, essentially, events do not happen to persons, persons happen to events – that is, the meaning a person gives to an event, and the response he or she makes to it, are more important than the specific nature of the event itself.

Humanistic astrology – This term was used also in the late 1960s to show that Rudhyar saw his approach to astrology in similar relation to the field of astrology as humanistic psychology was to the field of psychology. Humanistic psychology was a "third force" or alternative to Freudian psychoanalysis on one hand and statistical, experimental behaviorism on the other. Rudhyar's humanistic astrology was also a "third force," an alternative to both the traditional, predictive (fortune-telling) approach and a newly developing approach endeavoring to justify astrology statistically and to practice it according to statistical findings.

8) Astrology and statistics: Statistics deal only with large groups and have no bearing on individuals. Given the premise that in 75 out of 100 cases, astrological factor X produces or is associated with

Y situation, an astrologer dealing with a particular client has no reason to assume that the client will be one of the 75% rather than one of the 25%.

9) Astrology, academic "respectability," and licensing:

"In a field remarkable for its multiplicity of doctrines, none of which can be proven solely valid – for validity depends as much on the level of consciousness and the attitude of the client as on the technical knowledge of the astrologer – the possibility for some group to politically dominate the entire field is evident [viz. the AMA in medicine]... Obviously, many astrologers are not fit to affect the lives of their clients...But passing a state examination would not prove their ability to deal constructively with the multitude of psychological problems with which their clients may confront them."

"If popular and scientifically-oriented astrology today represents a 'mainstream,' then [the astrology] I have envisioned would be its 'counterculture.' It was meant as a challenge to the ordinary popular type of astrology to accept co-existence with a 'cosmopsychology' which is but part of a far wider movement of cultural and social transformation. An astrology taught in colleges, but divorced from such a movement and mainly intent on the development of a professionalism supported by national or state regulations would have, in my opinion, little meaning in the present world-crisis – a crisis of consciousness."

10) Transpersonal astrology:

Like the pioneers of the humanistic movement in psychology, Rudhyar acknowledged the limitations and omissions of a strictly humanistic approach to astrology. Although he had used the term transpersonal in 1930, he did not write specifically about transpersonal astrology until the early 1970s. Long before, however, whenever he wrote or spoke about the trans-Saturnian planets, Uranus, Neptune, and Pluto – whose "influences" conventional astrologers characterized as "malefic" – Rudhyar spoke about them as symbols of transformation, of going beyond the safe, secure realm of sociocultural convention and tradition and the circumference of individual selfhood (frames of reference symbolized by Saturn).

Transpersonal astrology addresses itself to the needs of individuals who realize that mere satisfaction – the growth and fulfillment of their individuality at a strictly personal or cultural level – is not an end in itself.

We usually think we are acting futureward when we try to actualize our birth-potentials, but what is actualized is mainly a prolongation, and usually only a superficially modified repetition, of our genetic and sociocultural past. The possibility of reaching a transindividual level forces us to choose between allegiance to a past we seek to fulfill in our own personal way and a future evolutionary state requiring radical transformation.

While a person-centered or humanistic approach is a tool for helping a person develop his or her birth-potentials (including the potentiality for individualized selfhood) harmoniously along socioculturally acceptable lines, transpersonal astrology tries to evoke for the individual eager for self-transcendence the possibility of **using** every circumstance, event, tension, and crisis as a means to overcome the inertia of his or her past, of social and mental habits, and above all, of the resistance of the "I" (the principle of individuality) to anything that would undermine its centralizing and controlling authority – that is, a radical transformation based on the realization that the "I" is a functional part of a much greater whole. Such a realization should form the foundation, not so much for a "giving up" of the "I," but for the self-consecration of the "I" to the performance of its dharma within and on behalf of the greater whole.

Transpersonal astrology is not "esoteric astrology," nor is it based on some sort of "soul chart." The same birth chart is the foundation for both a humanistic and transpersonal interpretation. It represents what a human organism starts from, the "givens" of his or her life. Generically, the human being has the possibility of becoming a person (sociocultural level), then a self-actualizing, autonomous individual, and eventually of growing beyond the state of strictly individual selfhood.

The birth chart is actually a "snapshot" of the state of the solar system (seen from a particular place on earth) at the time a human being is born. It is a moment in an immense continuum of activity involving all celestial factors and implying both the historical past and future momentum of their movements. Likewise, a human being is also a small area of space in the midst of the immense wave which is the evolution of mankind. It is an area into which a vast number of ancestral and sociocultural currents of psychic, mental, and spiritual forces converge. The humanistic approach concentrates on this convergence of factors shown by the birth chart as a formula for personality integration and fulfillment. The transpersonal approach concentrates on the dynamic process of transformation implied in the birth chart and its future movement (progressions).

The humanistic approach concentrates on horizontal relationships (relationships between entities operating at the same level – one's ancestors and family [biological level]; peers, associates, friends, lovers, spouses, and so on [sociocultural or individual level]. The transpersonal approach, on the other hand, concentrates on vertical relationships – that is, on the relationship between an individual (lesser whole) and the greater whole (in one sense humanity and the planet earth, in another the spiritual Quality and the Soul Field).

11) Transpersonal astrology and the transmutation of karma into dharma:

Karma represents the inertia of past patterns and currents of energies
- in terms of one's ancestors and genetic background (biological level)
- in terms of the past of one's society and culture (sociocultural level)
- in terms of one's past decisions and actions (individual level)

- in terms of the relative successes or failures of one's predecessor personalities in relation to the Soul Field (transindividual level)

Dharma represents the potential meaning and purpose the greater whole (humanity or the Soul Field) has invested in the birth of a new human being. It is what the newborn could do for humanity and what it will help him or her to do, if help is possible. The inertia of karma, however, may force merely a repetition of old patterns. Such a repetition would be almost inevitable if there were no possibility of the greater whole deliberately interacting with the lesser whole, the human being.

The transpersonal way is that path on which karma is transmuted into dharma: the inertia of the individual's past is **used** to fulfill a need of humanity. Along that way, crises serve to challenge the individual to stop acting as a creature of the past and to become a creator of the future – or rather, to become a focusing agent through whom humanity (or the Soul Field) is able to fulfill a particular, limited purpose.

Uranus, Neptune, and Pluto symbolize three steps or stages on the transpersonal way:
- some kind of crisis that reveals the inability of a strictly humanistic or person-centered approach to "solve" one's problems (Uranus)
- the process of becoming objective to forces of the past which condition one's actions, feelings, and thoughts; of deconditioning and severance (Neptune)

- a process of complete catharsis and repolarization – that is, the formation and empowerment of a new set of images polarizing one's mind and life – and rebirth (Pluto).

12) Astrological cycles symbolizing collective and planetary development:

As the possibilities for personal or individual growth or transformation are to a great extent defined by the stage of collective (generic and archetypal) human development, astrological symbols of long cycles can be of significant help in understanding the possibilities implied in our collective situation:

a) Hindu chronology speaks of multiples of a great cycle of 4,320,000 years, the lengths of four ages proceeding according to a descending arithmetic progression: *Satya Yuga* (4 units), *Trêtya Yuga* (3 units), *Dvâpara Yuga* (2 units), *Kali Yuga* (1 unit – 432,000 years). For Rudhyar, this cycle represents the involution of a spiritual impulse, which "decays" as it becomes increasingly "involved" in matter and loses its initial purity. *Kali Yuga*, the Dark Age, whose first 5,000 years ended in 1898 A.D., is not only the end of a great cycle, but also the period of gestation of a new humanity leading to the birth of a new Golden Age (*Satya Yuga*).

b) In a more limited sense, astrologically speaking, the 26,000-year cycle of precession of the equinoxes and its twelve subdivisions or Ages (Piscean, Aquarian, and so on) refer to the evolution of the planet earth and mankind. Thus the now-ending Piscean Age – the beginning of which Rudhyar puts at about 97-100 B.C. – marked the beginning not only of an Age, but of a complete 26,000-year cycle.

For Rudhyar, the keynote of the 26,000-year cycle that ended when the Piscean Age began was **cultivation**; the keynote of the present cycle, **universalization**.

What Rudhyar calls the Christ-Impulse constitutes the dynamizing, polarizing impulse, not only for the Piscean Age, but for the entire 26,000-year cycle. During the Piscean Age it was polarized by (or found its matrix for development in) the image of Caesar – the conqueror and administrator, the material, psychological counterpart to Jesus's revelation that "the kingdom of heaven is within you." Since the time of Christ, the Christ-Impulse has been "involving" itself into human substance. Thus, the first phase of this 26,000-year cycle has been one of both transcendent idealism and conflict. It was embodied in the European culture-cycle during the Christian era there, its prelude having begun about 600 B.C.

For Rudhyar, the Aquarian Age will not begin until about 2060 A.D., but the transition toward it (a "seed period" of one tenth of an Age) began about 1844-46. In 1844, the Persian prophet, the Bab, announced the end of an age and the impending appearance of a divine manifestation who would sound the creative "tone" of a new era of human evolution. Nineteen years later, Baha'u'llah declared himself to be this manifestation and founded the Baha'i Faith – actually a program for global organization based on divine revelation. Polarizing the Baha'i image of world order came the communist image projected by Marx, whose *Communist Manifesto* was published in 1848. Both movements represent firsts at outlining a truly global organization – one based on spiritual principles, the other on atheistic materialism and control of the means of producing goods. The accent on globality and humanitarian ideals also was symbolized by the discovery of the planet Neptune in 1846.

As the Aquarian Age will be the second period of the 26,000-year cycle, it should witness a substantiation (the keynote of phase 2 of any cycle) of the Christ-Impulse. But much collective karma – of religious dogmatism and materialistic reaction against it – must be neutralized and overcome, perhaps especially in the first half of the coming Age.

c) While the Ages of the precessional cycle refer to cyclic developments affecting the growth and dissolution of culture-wholes proper, the process of civilization is keyed to a 10,000-year rhythm symbolized by multiple cycles of Uranus, Neptune, and Pluto. The successive conjunctions of Pluto and Neptune at about 500-year intervals define significant sub-rhythms in this process.

Because Pluto's orbit is highly elongated and Neptune's nearly circular, twice in each Pluto/Neptune cycle Pluto passes inside the orbit of Neptune. As this occurs, Pluto and Neptune move at about the same rate, so their relationship remains relatively the same for nearly a century. Since about 1941, Pluto and Neptune have been in sextile – an aspect of about 60 degrees symbolizing **organization**. While such a long aspect occurs about every 250 years, it is not always a sextile following (rather than preceding) a conjunction. The "Enlightenment" period of the American and French revolutions occurred toward the end of a century-long trine (an aspect symbolizing the expression of creative vision). Toward the end of the last long sextile like ours, Constantinople fell to the Turks, and many Byzantine scholars fled to northern Italy where they sparked the Humanist movement and the Italian Renaissance. In our present long sextile (which will end around 2030). Tibet has been overtaken by the Chinese, and many Buddhist scholars and Tibetan lamas have emigrated to the West.

The function of a period whose "signature" is such a long sextile is to organize in form what was released under the preceding Pluto/Neptune conjunction (1891-92). During that time, the World Parliament of Religions was held in Chicago, and for the first time Americans heard some of the Eastern wisdom directly from learned Asian teachers themselves. Technological inventions of the last decade of the nineteenth century are too numerous to mention here – but perhaps most significant among them was the discovery of radium by Mme. Curie in 1898.

d) Astrologically, our century has been one of crisis and transition. Between 1892 and 2000 all interplanetary cycles end and begin anew (at least once, some several times because their periods are short enough). Most significant have been, and will be, the Pluto/Uranus conjunctions of 1966-67 and the Neptune/Uranus conjunctions of 1993. While the period surrounding the Pluto/Uranus conjunctions emphasized the liberating, revolutionary symbolism of Uranus and Aquarius (there was a "stellium" of seven planets in Aquarius in 1962), the period surrounding the Neptune/Uranus conjunctions of 1993 will emphasize the, consolidating, more reactionary symbolism of Capricorn – although Capricorn also symbolizes the "great hope of rebirth and self-renewal, the glad tidings of Christ-birth" (the Neptune/Uranus conjunction itself occurs in Capricorn and there will be a stellium of seven planets in Capricorn in 1994). Between now and then, Libra (1981-83 – interpersonal and international relationships and diplomacy) and Sagittarius (1983-88 – expansion, formulation of philosophy or ideology) will be highlighted in turn.

Rudhyar often mentions a remark made by a theosophist-occultist who was a significant exemplar for him early in his life, "There is nothing one can do **to** *Kali Yuga*, but there is a great deal one can do **in** *Kali Yuga*." For Rudhyar, exactly what happens as our century ends and the transition to the much awaited (and often overly idealized and utopianized) Aquarian Age accelerates is of relatively little importance. What counts is the quality of mind, involvement, and response individuals offer to the challenges of their lives and times. He often bewails the young generations' ignorance of and disinterest in history, for he feels that opportunities for transformation now are not totally different from what they were at major turning points in the past. Individuals living then, however, lacked the truly global perspective we can have today, and there were not publicly available to them the occult esoteric principles which today can give structure, objectivity, and clarity to an understanding of evolutionary processes.

For Rudhyar, **the one** essential requirement for collective or individual transformation is the development of a new mentality – a new mind able to meet and envision the future because it is free from the "ghosts" of the past: a mind consciously formed and structured to be a clear lens for focusing transpersonal activity; a mind consciously accepting its evolutionary function to be the vessel in which spirit and matter can become harmonized.

3. PSYCHOLOGY

1) The cornerstone of Rudhyar's approach to psychology is his presentation of four levels of human functioning. These four levels are:
    a) The **biological level**, at which human beings operate as strictly biological organisms dominated by the exigencies and compulsions of life. The principle of individuality (ONE or SELF) manifests as variations on the dominant type of the race or people to which a particular human being belongs.
    b) The **sociocultural level**, at which human beings operate as **persons** within complex culture-whole's, almost totally subservient to collective frames of reference. The need of the human biological organism to adjust itself to psychosocial pressures produces the **ego**, the function of which is to be the interface between biology and culture. The ego gives rise to the "feeling-of-being-I," which is a reflection of the principle of individuality at the sociocultural level. The main drive of the ego is for psychosocial security; it is motivated by fear and guilt and strives to attain personal happiness through the approval and admiration of others.
    c) The **individual level**, at which persons, having questioned and become objective to the taken-for-granted symbols and images of their cultures, develop autonomous, independent minds and wills. The principle of

individuality manifests as individual selfhood; the "I" is motivated largely by pride in its uniqueness and in its power over circumstances (internal or external), other people, and objects.
d) The **transindividual level**, at which individuals, having transcended their selfish separativeness and consecrated themselves to the service of the whole (humanity or the planetary organism of the earth) operate at the level of the Pleroma.

These four levels are linked by "functions of transition" or "seed functions":
    a) The seed function between the biological and sociocultural levels is **sex**. In its strictly procreative aspect, sex belongs to the biological level; yet unlike other biological functions (such as breathing and eating) its operation is not absolutely crucial for the continuing existence of a particular organism. Moreover, other biological functions are intra-organic, while sex is inter-organic: it requires the interaction of two organisms. In animals, the relationship between potentially mating organisms is seasonally controlled; in human beings it is controlled and regulated by culture, by religious and secular paradigms and mores. Hence, "life, through sex, develops into culture."
    b) The function of transition between the sociocultural and individual levels is the **analytical**

intellect, which separates itself from and dissects situations and experiences atomistically. As it develops, it becomes a powerful tool facilitating the process of "liberation" from both the instinctual compulsions of biology and the collective psychism of sociocultural imperatives and taboos. For Rudhyar, the separative and atomizing activity of the intellectual aspect of the mind is a necessary phase in collective and individual human evolution; just as, in logic, the antithesis is an integral part of a syllogism leading from the thesis to the synthesis. But it should be considered only a transitory stage between the compulsive biopsychic activity of the archaic, relatively unconscious and essentially collective mind, and the individually conscious, yet also holistic and unanimistic activity of the pleromic mind which all human consciousnesses **potentially** interpenetrate. Similarly, the "I-feeling" itself also should be regarded as only a transitory experience; it forms the necessary basis for an antithetic kind of mentality and worldview which eventually should lead to a new synthesis represented by the transindividual level.

c) The function of transition between the individual and transpersonal levels is what Rudhyar calls **selfconsecration to the whole** and the development of the **mind of wholeness**. It is the process of transformation making the I-center of the personality attuned to the functional nature of its uniqueness, its potential contribution to the whole, and translucent to the light and spiritual Quality of the Soul Field. Much of Rudhyar's recent work is concerned with clarifying what is implied in this Path of transformation (at least in its first phases) and helping Westerners to orient themselves toward it realistically and without glamor, in terms of fundamental principles. Concentrating the mind upon these principles should, if done regularly, intently, and perseveringly, develop the mind of wholeness. Yet this transformation requires more than deep feelings and a clear mind. It demands a persistent and steady, though resilient and pliable, will. Traditional disciplines and practices having an exotic or fascinating appeal may steady and test the will-to-transformation; but they also may give rise to a subtle kind of ego-pride (particularly at the level of collective psychism sustaining any religious or esoteric group). Ultimate success requires a truly individualized and independent will that does not require collective support. Above all, it demands humility and nonattachment to any result.

2) Rudhyar's approach to psychology can be characterized as a combination of *Jnana* and *Karma yoga*: *Jnana yoga* in that it seeks to foster and requires the development of a clear, objective mind sufficiently individualized to operate in relative independence from biological urges and collective

fashions, imperatives, and taboos – a mind capable of thinking and of understanding the human condition (including one's own) in terms of basic historical, hierarchical, and evolutionary principles; *Karma yoga* in that, while Rudhyar's philosophy is essentially mental, he is not an intellectual and does not advocate an intellectual approach to living. For him, motion – activity – is the essence of being. In his approach to psychology, will and activity are as important as feelings and emotions.

3) In relation to particular actions, however, Rudhyar often asks the question, who – or what – is performing the act? This question points out Rudhyar's belief that the role of culture in individual living is far more significant than contemporary psychologies allow. For him, a culture is **not** an aggregate of otherwise separate human beings who "choose" to relate themselves to one another through a common way of life. Culture is **prior** to any person or individual born into it, and only through culture can a human being become a person, then an individual. Culture molds and shapes the mind and feeling-nature, at first along collective lines. Especially inherent in Euro-American culture today, there are conflicts to challenge persons to emerge from the dominance of its collective psychism – and the integrity of its collective psychism is fast disintegrating as accelerated individualization undermines what once were integral, powerful religious and cultural symbols. Until a person emerges fully from the culture's collective psychism, it is the culture – its paradigms, symbols,

and images – that condition and operate through personal feelings, thoughts, and deeds.

Yet substituting an alien culture's way of living, feeling and thinking for one's natal culture's does not necessarily constitute individualization; on the contrary, it may merely make one subservient to a different collective frame of reference from the one into which one was born. However, familiarity with another culture's practices, special vocabulary, and way of life may be constructive if it helps one become more objective to the collective psychism of one's natal culture, and if it provides one's individualizing mind with new and more adequate terms in which to formulate one's worldview. But if immersion in another culture's collective psychism is premature or unassimilable, a reactionary backlash may result – one may revert or regress to a less sophisticated stage or unthinking fundamentalism of one's natal culture.

4) For Rudhyar, another interpenetration of collective and individual development results in the production of characteristic types of persons and individuals at various stages of cultural development. For him, cultures develop according to a dialectical pattern of thesis, antithesis, synthesis. During the second or antithetical phase, following the thesis or tribal phase, a culture's development follows a fourfold pattern, which parallels the four levels of human development presented above.

Each period of culture produces a characteristic type of person that manifests in a positive, negative (passive), and transcendent aspect. Each type requires a characteristic path of individualization represented by the transcendent aspect of the type. The path of emergence conditions the essential characteristics of the emerging individual, and it is usually connected with the transcendent ideals of the culture's dominant religion. The lives and deeds of these individuals, in turn, affect the social and cultural fabric, especially as the process of individualization accelerates and the culture's collective psychism breaks down. While these types operate historically, they are still active today as prototypes conditioning personal and individual psychology.

a) The first period of cultural development is concerned primarily with vigorous physical activity, possession of land and of the means of production. The positive dominant type is the Warrior (the *Kshatriya* caste in India) in whom muscular energy, daring, and procreative power prove and maintain authority. The negative of the type is the soldier, serf, or slave, who in the tribal age (thesis) partook of the psychic unanimity of the tribe and obeyed an inner compulsion associated with the tribal god, but who now obeys the outer will of the dominant lord or master. The path to individualization for this type is also one of action and conquest, but action and conquest for a transcendent purpose. This transcendent type is exemplified in India by King Rama, in Europe by the Knight-Crusader epitomized by King Arthur. This type is closely associated with the ideal of chivalry and courtly love in Europe, with the perfect husband-wife relationship in India (Rama and Sita). Krishna stands as the highest symbol of emergence into individual selfhood through transcendent action performed for and as the supreme Self: action without regard for the fruits of action. As the type degenerates, the Knight-Crusader becomes merely the conquistador, whose fateful search for gold breeds violence, cruelty, and greed.

b) The second period of cultural development during the antithesis phase is primarily concerned with consolidating, preserving, cultivating, and refining the values acquired during the previous period; with the development of institutions molding collective behavior, feeling, and thinking. The positive of the type is the Priest Philosopher (India's *Brahmin* caste), the clergy backed by committees of scholars and academics, able to enforce its decrees with excommunication, imprisonment, or death. The Philosopher-Priest also functions as statesman and diplomat, thus facilitating peaceful intercultural contacts. The negative of the type is the religious devotee compelled to fit into the dominant socio-religious scheme because of personal insecurity and uncertainty – a relatively recent development. This type individualizes via the path of the mystic or compassionate saint – in India, the Forest Philosophers of the Upanishad period, the yogi or *sannyasin*; in Europe, St. Francis and a host of mystics: all individuals who emerge from the mass patterns of religion and are reborn through an individual experience of spirit. Another aspect of this type is the religious reformer who individualizes through the power of moral rebellion (for example, Luther and Calvin in Europe). In India, the greatest exemplar of this path was Gautama Buddha, who urged transcendence of the caste system and Hindu ritual. With Jesus, love as the supreme law transcended all religious laws, and the subjective feeling of union with the Father transcended all racial and dogmatic boundaries. This type degenerates when the mystic becomes a militant fanatic (for example, militant orders participating in the Inquisition).

c) The third period witnesses the growth of trade, the spread of interpersonal and intercultural relationships, the expansion of production, and the stimulation of intellectual faculties. The dominant type of the Trader or Merchant (India's *Vaishya* caste) – a class of tradesmen, professionals, industrialists, bankers, and international financiers. The essential characteristic of the type is a personal restlessness both feeding upon and fueling the intellect. As cultural and religious exclusivism breaks down, so does the power of collective psychism; each human being must find his or her own security: every man a law unto himself. This, idealized, becomes democracy. The negative of the type is a mass of workers and passive consumers, mere wage-earners without any security whatsoever. The transcendent aspect of the type is the adventurer, the heroes of science or medicine, the visionaries who sacrifice or dedicate their lives to opening new lines of trade, new continents, new horizons. Such geniuses are often human beings in whom abnormal psychology turns creative, persons who use the energy of their frustrations, complexes, and suffering to transcend the norm and emerge as individuals beyond the boundaries of society. They use conflict and struggle evolutionarily, for performing creative acts which are seeds for the future. As the type degenerates, it produces individuals who feed upon and profit from the pervasive cultural dysfunction.

d) The fourth period begins on a foundation of social and individual chaos. The negative of the type is the Money-Conditioned individual who achieves a degree of security in a dog-eat-dog world. The anonymous social power of money consumes the minds and passions of all, whether wealthy or without financial means. The first manifestation of a positive of the type is the Man of Service (analogous to India's *Shudra* caste) – the martyr to a visionary social cause (e.g., the Bab of Persia, Lenin, Gandhi) – the symbol of utter self-surrender, service, and sacrifice. The passive aspect of the type is the Technician – the engineers, production managers, efficiency experts, economists, and statisticians who serve the industrial and electronic machinery of corporate society. The transcendent aspect of the type is the Seed Man or Woman, the creative individual who deliberately and consciously dedicates his or her individuality to the service of humanity, its spirit-emanated and spirit-oriented evolutionary goal.

5) The challenge facing most Westerners today is to emerge from the sway of the dominant social images of dysfunctional individualism and egalitarianism. The great paradox is that most people demanding individual rights are not individuals at all, but personal egos strongly conditioned by a collective image of individualism.

For Rudhyar, the **ego** is not an entity but a complex of interrelated activities, the function of which is to make the adjustments necessary to maintain the biological organism amid the psycho-social pressures in which it has to operate. The ego is conditioned by both biology (the organism's temperament or biopsychic type) and culture – the social and religious images, symbols, imperatives, and taboos active at the level of collective psychism. It operates as a kind of floating center of gravity in answer to external pressures. It is moved primarily by insecurity and fear. That it can develop and give rise to the feeling of "being I" is a reflection of the **potentiality** of individual selfhood.

The "real I" disengaged from family, social, and cultural patterns is what Rudhyar calls the actual center of the "mandala of personality." It is not identical with the ego, but it tries to use the ego's functional activities for its own purpose. While the ego is moved by insecurity and fear, the "I" at first is motivated primarily by pride. It is SELF (or ONE) operating at the individual level.

"The seers-philosophers of old India have given various names to this Principle. When considered as a 'Presence' (an insubstantial 'breath') within a human being, they spoke of it as ***atman***. In relation to the whole universe, they usually gave it the name ***brahman***. The great revelation that took form in the ancient Upanishads was that *atman* and *brahman* were essentially identical. The same power of integration, the same mysterious, actually unreachable and ineffable Presence, was inherent in all living beings; and as life itself was but one of its particular modes of operation, the whole universe and all it contains were alive."

"As a Principle of power of integration, SELF is present everywhere, but its mode of operation differs at each level of existence. Since a human being functions and is conscious at several levels, SELF has to be understood in a human being in several ways – biologically, socioculturally, individually, and, eventually, transindividually. It is best, however, not to speak of a 'biological self' or an 'individual self,' but instead of a biological, sociocultural, and individual **state of selfhood**. Biological selfhood has a generic and, in the usual sense of the term, unconscious character; sociocultural selfhood has a collective character; and individual selfhood is achieved by undergoing a long and arduous process of individualization. The process of human evolution has so far consisted in bringing the sense of self from the unconscious darkness of the biological nature to a condition of ever clearer and inclusive consciousness through the development of ever finer, more complex cultures and of ever more responsive conscious individuals. A still more inclusive and universal realization of SELF should be achieved when the state beyond individual consciousness is reached – what I have called the Pleroma state of consciousness." (*Astrology of Transformation*, pp. 78-79)

6) For Rudhyar, a psychological complex is a set of ideas, feelings, sensations, memories, etc. which have acquired rigidity and relative independence from the will – that is, from the centralizing capacity consciously to mobilize one's energies and act in a particular, deliberate way. Complexes are based essentially on the memory of defeat – whether the memory is strictly personal in nature or is based on a subconscious memory of previous collective defeats. They originate in a person's **reaction** to a situation in which he or she **feels** defeated. The complex grows in strength and inertia as subsequent situations similarly experienced confirm the feeling of defeat.

A sense of defeat – and therefore psychological complexes – is possible because we live in a culture that envisions life as a battle between opposing forces. For Rudhyar, "Where force meets force, there man must ultimately be defeated; the irresistibly moving forces of nature, either in the physical world or in the psychic realm of the unconscious whose depths are unending and unfathomable, will always, in the long run, defeat the forces of humanity and especially of an individual person alone…"

"Yet there is an alternative. Once we realize that the essential purpose of life for man is the progressive actualization of inner powers inherent in the creative spirit within the individual, the whole outlook is changed…Consider an individual permeated with the belief that he is born in order to develop his inner powers through storm and sunshine, pain and happiness alike…If he is beaten in any meeting with the mighty energies of nature (inner or outer), such an individual will not acquire a 'sense of defeat,' however bruised and hurt he might be, as long as he may feel that he has learnt and grown as a personality out of the tragic experience…[Such an] individual, setting into operation the inner powers of his being, buries the dead and creates new values." (*Astrological Study of Psychological Complexes*, p. 5-6)

7) The aim of a psychotherapy based on Rudhyar's multileveled approach to psychology would be to try to unravel the threads of psychological complexes, not merely to uncover their apparent causes, but to try to evoke an understanding of their meaning – that is, what they reveal about the level at which one is operating and therefore the evolutionary possibilities inherent in that position.

From Rudhyar's point of view, one can move forward only from where one stands, although some positions make forward motion easier than others. Some stances may require a temporary "strategic retreat" that should not be interpreted as a permanent policy of defeat or withdrawal. In a deeper sense, however, for Rudhyar the true "way" is neither forward nor back, but **through**:

"**Through** – small, yet mighty word! Everything is what it is through its opposite. Man experiences through nature. He rises through nature. Not against, but through…The hand passes through the water. It experiences the water, the fluidity of it; yet it emerges from it, still a hand – the integrity of a hand, **plus** consciousness from the experience. Consciousness is throughness. It is born of thoroughness of experiencing…Having experienced to the full, man is 'through' with this particular field of experience, because he has gained consciousness of himself, the experiencer…"

"Nature is everything through which man must gain consciousness, and through consciousness an immortal form of emptiness, chalice for the downpour of the Holy Spirit – the light of the Whole. Nature is everything that man must overcome in order to be more than only man. Overcoming is a passing through, not a dismissal. Nature is not to be dismissed before the experience; it is not to be shunned and fearfully avoided. It is to be met in contest within the limited field of the life-experiencer…Yet each of the contestants occupies the entire field. The only solution of the contest is for man to enter the whole of nature within the field of experience, to pierce through nature and, emerging from nature and the field, to continue his path toward an ever more total fullness of being…"

"As man knows himself through his contest with nature, so does nature realize itself whole by the light of man's victory. It is this light which alone illumines nature. This indeed is the destiny of all nature: that it can realize itself whole, and thus reach its own fulfillment, only if it is successfully overcome by the man whom it must oppose so that he might know himself by piercing it through, and knowing himself, illumine it by the light of that knowing. In this process nature acts as challenger. It challenges man, yet with the unconscious desire to be overcome by man."

"The field is limited. Each contestant fills it entirely. There is no way out for man save through and through – or back. To pierce through nature and move Godward – or to fall back, entangled in the fateful advance of natural energies toward chaos." (*An Astrological Triptych*, pp. 104-07)

APPENDIX I

SELECTED POEMS

by Dane Rudhyar

ROCKS

I have walked through cities, gardens and oases.
I have suffered through births, struggles and passions.
I have pulsated with the beat of the storms.
I have thrown my life open like a womb.
I have sung and sorrowed; I have dreamt and fought.
Every nerve of me has been scarred and blessed.

I face now the desert and the rocks.
They burn with sun. They fever with light.
They are bare and solemn, live with rattling death.
They tower, yet have no scorn.
Though no sound comes from their tortured peace,
with poignancy and love they speak.
Oh, these words they utter
they burn through, they hollow, they soothe.
They are open like eyes
and closed like tombs.
They are fragrant with heat.
They are dull and sullen
and my heart wilts
before the grandeur of their silences.

Take me, loveless rocks, into your sepulcher
that lives and surges with passion greater
than all the lusciousness of oases.
Take me who have become your peer in barrenness,
whom life has stunned into ecstatic death.
Oh! take me that am but a mortal
and fain would partake of your agelessness!

I have walked through cities, gardens and horizons.
I have suffered through births, loves and the end of love.
Let me rest in you with the peace of stone,
that I too might dream endless dreams,
cold by night, burning by day –
dreams strong and old,
foundations of new earths.

ULTIMATE STANCE

1.

I have captured the mighty sun
within my armor, formed and strong.
I knew his glamor, his dazzling;
and I rose above his golden lure.
I sacrifice unto my star
through nights consecrated and clear
where my heart encompasses
the wholeness of crystalline space.

Through the seried months of the year
my earth revolved around the sun
compelled by his insistent might;
and the wholeness of me was spread
over long weeks of wandering.
But now in my own self I stand,
my soul riveted to the Star
round which centered and firm I move,
whole within the span of the day.

And in the uttermost alone,
secure within my high gates,
where neither earth nor sun ever
have power to scatter my self
through long revolving day and year,
there, at last, I am that I am,
indivisible and constant,
a pin-point of eternity.

2.

Now comes the moment of Soul.
Years have passed
of search, of contingencies,
of hopes and still-born deeds.
It has been a good fight, clean and fair.
Now, as if death were near,
I stand facing the wall that may open,
strong at heart, ready for the confrontation.
I may fall
yet am not afraid of failure.
I may win
yet court no victory.
I have but one aim:
to fulfill my destiny
whatever the means, whatever the fruits,
whatever the path.
I contemplate the past from which I emerged:
my record.
Nothing seems useless now,
nothing wasted, nothing that could be otherwise.

Satisfaction?
This would be meaningless.
There is never "enough";
but what is
IS.
To that I assent.

Utter calmness, indifference even.
It does not matter. It is not "matter".
It is not one thing or the other.
It is I, that am all.
For this minute I am all,
because poised in destiny,
unified in destiny,
a uniqueness which is Allness,
a void transparent to fullness.

It is all there.
It matters not that I cannot spell the names.
When all names are told at once,
they become meaningless;
they become power.
Because I am power that is total,
I desire nothing.
How could I?
To desire
is to admit lack of power.
But to him that is power as destiny,
death is open.
He marches into it
towards the Soul.

I am marching on, my friends,
into my space and my silence.
It is as if I were all open,
open like an ever-receding sky.
It is so quiet
I can sense the heart beats
of multitudes of destinies.
I am poised in all destinies.

APPENDIX II

BIBLIOGRAPHY

Published volumes by Dane Rudhyar

1) *Claude Debussy et son oevre* (Durand et Cie., Paris, 1913)
2) *Rhapsodies* (Impremerie Beauregard, Ottawa, 1919)
3) *The Rebirth of Hindu Music* (The Theosophical Publishing House, Adyar, 1928; Samuel Weiser, New York, 1979)
4) *Toward Man* (Seven Arts, Carmel, 1938)
5) *Art as Release of Power* (Hamsa Publications, Carmel, 1930)
6) *Astrology of Personality* (Lucis Publishing Co., New York, 1936; David McKay, Philadelphia, 1946; Servire B.V., The Netherlands, 1963; Doubleday, New York, 1970)
7) *New Mansions for New Men* (Lucis Publishing Co., New York, 1938; David McKay, Philadelphia, 1946; Servire B.V., The Netherlands, 1971; Hunter House, Pomona, 1978)
8) *White Thunder* (Hazel Dreiss Editions, Santa Fe, 1938; Seed Center, Palo Alto, 1976)
9) *The Faith that Gives Meaning to* Victory (Foundation for Human Integration, Reseda, 1942)
10) *The Pulse of Life* (David McKay, Philadelphia, 1943; Servire B.V., The Netherlands, 1963; Shambhala Publications, Berkeley, 1970; retitled Astrological Signs: The Pulse of Life, Shambhala

Publications, Boulder, 1978; Raven Dreams Press, Boulder, 2023)
11) *Seeds of Plenitude* (Rydal Press, Santa Fe, 1943)
12) *The Moon: The Cycles and Fortunes of Life* (David McKay, Philadelphia, 1946; later revised and retitled The Lunation Cycle)
13) *Modern Man's Conflicts* (Philosophical Library, New York, 1948)
14) *Gifts of the Spirit* (New Age Publishing Co., Los Angeles, 1956; later revised and incorporated into Triptych)
15) *Fire Out of the Stone* (Servire B.V., The Netherlands, 1963)
16) *Rhythm of Human Fulfillment* (Seed Ideas Publications, San Jacinto, 1966; Seed Center, Palo Alto, 1973)
17) *An Astrological Study of Psychological Complexes* (self-published, San Jacinto, 1966; Servire B.V., The Netherlands, 1973; Shambhala Publications, Berkeley, 1976)
18) *Of Vibrancy and Peace* (Servire B.V., The Netherlands, 1967)
19) *The Lunation Cycle* (Shambhala Publications, Berkeley, 1971)
20) *Triptych: Gifts of the Spirit – The Way Through – The Illumined Road* (Servire B.V., The Netherlands, 1968; retitled *An Astrological Triptych*, ASI Publishers, New York, 1971; Aurora Press, New York, 1983)
21) *Practice of Astrology* (Servire B.V., The Netherlands, 1968; Penguin Books, New York, 1971; Shambhala Publications, Berkeley, 1978)

22) *Birth Patterns for a New Humanity* (Servire B.V., The Netherlands, 1969; retitled Astrological Timing: The Transition to the New Age, Harper, New York, 1972)

23) *Planetarization of Consciousness* (Servire B.V., The Netherlands, 1970; Harper, New York, 1972; ASI Publishers, New York, 1977; Aurora Press, New York, 1983)

24) *Person-Centered Astrology* (Originally published as six booklets entitled "Humanistic Astrology Series," CSA Press, Lakemont, 1970-71; first volume edition CSA, 1972; ASI Publishers, New York, 1980; Aurora Press, New York, 1983)

25) *Directives for New Life* (Seed Publications, Railroad Flat, 1971)

26) *Astrological Themes for Meditation* (CSA Press, Lakemont, 1972; later incorporated into Astrological Insights into the Spiritual Life)

27) *My Stand on Astrology* (Seed Center, Palo Alto, 1972; later incorporated into From Humanistic to Transpersonal Astrology)

28) *The Astrological Houses* (Doubleday, New York, 1972)

29) *Rania* (Unity Press, Santa Cruz, 1973; Avon, New York, 1975)

30) *An Attempt at Formulating Minimal Requirements for the Practice of Natal Astrology* (Portland Astrology Center, Portland, 1973)

31) *A Seed* (Seed Publications, Railroad Flat, 1973)

32) *An Astrological* Mandala (Random House, New York, 1973; Raven Dreams Press, 2023)

33) *We Can Begin Again – Together* (Omen Communications, Tucson, 1974; Rudhyar Books & Tapes, Palo Alto, 1976)
34) *The Astrology of America's Destiny* (Random House, New York, 1974)
35) *The Astrological Approach to Inner Fulfillment* (Inner Forum, Boise, 1974)
36) *Occult Preparations for a New Age* (Quest Books, Wheaton, 1975)
37) *From Humanistic to Transpersonal Astrology* (Seed Center, Palo Alto, 1975)
38) *The Sun is Also a Star* (Dutton, New York, 1975; retitled *The Galactic Dimension of Astrology*, ASI Publishers, 1980; Aurora Press, New York, 1983)
39) *Astrology and the Modern Psyche* (CRCS Publications, Reno, 1976)
40) *Zodiacal Signatures* (Stellar Energy Exchange, Guerneville, 1976; later incorporated into *Astrological Insights into the Spiritual Life*)
41) *Ariete* (Armenia Editore, Milano, 1977)
42) *Culture, Crisis and Creativity* (Quest Books, Wheaton, 1977)
43) *Paths to the Fire* (Hermes Press, Ferndale, 1978)
44) *Beyond Individualism: The Psychology of Transformation* (Quest Books, Wheaton, 1979)
45) *Astrological Insights into the Spiritual Life* (ASI Publishers, New York, 1979; Aurora Press, New York, 1983)
46) *Astrology of Transformation* (Quest Books, Wheaton, 1980)

47) *Astrological Aspects*, with Leyla Raël (ASI Publishers, New York, 1979; Aurora Press, New York, 1983)
48) *Rudhyar: Person and Destiny* (written 1981, as yet unpublished)
49) *The Magic of Tone and the Art of Music* (Shambhala Publications, Boulder, 1982)
50) *Beyond Personhood* (RITA, Palo Alto, 1983)
51) *Rhythm of Wholeness* (Quest Books, Wheaton, 1983)

www.ingramcontent.com/pod-product-compliance
Lightning Source LLC
Chambersburg PA
CBHW060842050426
42453CB00008B/787